> # Vision without action is nothing.

It's one thing to have a big dream, but it's another to actually action it.

"

@lisamessenger

Visions & Actions
2020, *Collective Hub*

All rights reserved. No part of this book may be reproduced in any form or by any means, electronic or mechanical, including photocopying, recording or by any information or retrieval, without prior permission in writing from the publisher. Under the Australian Copyright Act 1968 (the Act), a maximum of one chapter or 10 per cent of the book, whichever is the greater, may be photocopied by any educational institution for its educational purposes provided that the education institution (or the body that administers it) has given a remuneration notice to Copyright Agency Limited (CAL) under the Act. Any views and opinions expressed herein are strictly the author's own and do not represent those of The Messenger Group. A CIP catalogue of this book is available from the National Library of Australia.

ISBN 978-0-6485872-6-2
First published in 2020 by The Messenger Group Pty Ltd

Project management, copywriting,
creative direction & design:
Emily Karamihas

Proofreading and editing:
Emily Ditchburn, Claire Hey & Alexandra English

Distribution enquiries:
Lisa Messenger, lisam@collectivehub.com

This is proudly a *Collective Hub* product,
collectivehub.com

Disclaimer

The content of this book is to serve as a general overview of matters of interest and is not intended to be comprehensive, nor does it constitute advice in any way. This book is a compilation of one person's ideas, concepts, ideologies, philosophies and opinions. You should carry out your own research and/or seek your own professional advice before acting or relying on any of the information displayed in this book. The author, The Messenger Group Pty Ltd and its related entities will not be liable for any loss or damage (financial or otherwise) that may arise out of your improper use of, or reliance on, the content of this book. You accept sole responsibility for the outcomes if you choose to adopt and/or use the ideas, concepts, ideologies, philosophies and opinions within the content of this book.

visions & actions

create and achieve your dream

COLLECTIVE HUB

> **It takes someone with a vision of the possibilities to attain new levels of experience. Someone with the courage to live his dreams.**

– Les Brown

contents

INTRODUCTION
6

SECTION ONE
HOW TO USE THIS JOURNAL
8

SECTION TWO
DAILY ACCOUNTABILITY
26

+ EXTRAS
316

introduction

Vision inspires action.

Action creates achievement.

So, what is vision?
It's mental clarity of your purpose, a driver to achieve your goals and dreams. Your vision creates energy, excitement, passion and commitment. It's the one *big* piece of the puzzle that follows you every step of your journey to living your best life. Having clear vision in life, career, relationships and your daily routine will unlock barriers and propel you on a path to your wildest dreams.

And, what is action?
Action is the process of doing something to achieve something! So, what steps are you taking to make your vision a reality? There's no vision without action and there's no action without vision. The two go hand in hand if you want to achieve your ultimate goals. Creating realistic, actionable steps every day will keep you accountable while creating and achieving whatever your vision may be.

Our **Visions & Actions** journal has been designed to guide you all the way from day-to-day routines, to big-picture goals and dreams. We've formulated these pages to give you the **best opportunities** to create success in the most realistic and practical ways. We've rallied all our tried and tested routines, rituals, practices, knowledge, advice and tips to ease you into this journey and provide you with all the tools needed to action, implement and **achieve!**

One of the greatest ways to turn your visions into action is through consistency. Remember, many small actions practised day after day, week after week and even year after year will all contribute to your big-picture goals and **ultimate vision**. As long as you stay true to your purpose and hold on to your passions, **anything is truly possible.**

We'd love to hear all about your plans, goals and visions — tag us in your journey **@collectivehub** so we can be inspired by you, too!

Lisa & the Collective Hub team xx

HOW TO
USE THIS JOURNAL

We recommend you approach the *Vision & Actions* journal step-by-step, day-by-day and month-by-month. Work through this journal from beginning to end as you would read a book.

In this journal, we unpack each of the steps needed to achieve, and provide you with a huge resource of tools and knowledge to help guide you in the most beneficial way through this journey. Read each point carefully and consider how you will approach each question, task or exercise.

There's no rush — remember to take your time! The questions are designed to make you think and reflect. Each of us is different and we digest questions/situations/moods/actions differently. Go at your own pace and take the necessary time to feel into each question. Think honestly about your answers or your actions.

It's also recommended that you come back to this section of the journal regularly to remind yourself that this is a journey and not an overnight quick fix. Let's get clear, concise and formulate *your* best strategy so you don't get lost on the way — you've got this and we're here to guide you and keep you on track.

WHY YOU'RE GOING TO LOVE THIS JOURNAL

Well, it's the kind of journal that isn't all about journalling. The questions within these pages are designed to be concise and considered and are all focused on two main points: visions and actions (obviously!). It's simple, really — work through the journal day-by-day, and at the end of each week there's a page dedicated to making sure you're on track. And then, for an added element of accountability, we've designed a monthly check-in, too. If you want to achieve, you absolutely have to stay accountable!

These pages will be like a shining light if you're feeling a little unmotivated or stuck. We're here to make sure that is quickly turned around and you're moving onwards and upwards.

The further you get into this journal, the more aligning your vision and strategising actions will become second nature. You'll begin to notice that these moments will naturally start becoming a part of your daily routine: checking in, aligning your vision and taking action!

So, let's delve into it and unpack each of the main areas in your daily routine.

VISION SETTING

Setting up your vision and creating a **clear and concise** picture of your outcome will be the biggest driver for a seamless journey to the finale. After listing and visualising your biggest goals for the next 12 months, we'll talk you through some of the techniques we practise to help you become **super clear** on both your vision and your actionable plans. Think fun exercises such as mind mapping and laddering, vision boarding and even manifesting. It's important to check in on all areas of your life, too, including the personal and emotional, not just your career or work!

VISION & ACTIONS ACCOUNTABILITY

The very best way to stay focused and on track is to create habits and routines. Checking in with the pages in this book will be one of them! Leave your Vision & Actions planner somewhere accessible, like on your bedside table or on the bench in your kitchen. Answer your daily questions while making your morning coffee or slurping up your cereal. Whatever works best for you — but just make sure you're coming back every day to track your progress, align your vision and tick off your actionables for that day! You are accountable for your daily check-in, so it's up to you to build this into your routine the best way that suits you. If you're serious about this and truly have the desire to create your best life — trust us, you'll find a way!

WEEKLY RECAPS

As mentioned a little earlier in these pages, the weekly recap is designed to keep you aligned and accountable. If you miss a day or two in your daily accountability practice, it's even more important to check in at the end of the week, reflect and note down any big moments from the previous seven days. The weekly recap also intends to set you up for the week ahead by asking thought-provoking questions about your progress, your plans, your goals and your actionables for the next seven days.

MONTHLY REVIEWS

These sections in your journal are an extension on the weekly recaps. Use your weekly recaps to choose the best and the worst situations and/or moments of each month and delve into them a little further. Write about your progress in your goals, how you visualised each of them, and list both the positive and negative learning experiences. Give yourself time to relive your weekly goals and what you did to achieve them, or how you failed to achieve them. Write, draw, scribble – whatever works for you. Monthly reviews are designed to inspire and motivate, manifest and transition you to a brand new month with lots of new and exciting ideas and perspectives, while still keeping your vision strong!

WHY YOUR VISIONS MATTER SO MUCH

Within each Daily Accountability page, you'll notice questions prompting you for today's visions. As you'll know by now, what you visualise and action will eventuate, so this is important.

These questions on your daily visions — in life, career, relationships and health and wellness — will set your day up in the best way possible.

Having these mini daily visions to think about and reflect on will help so much in contributing energy, positive mindset, confidence and determination to your bigger goals and visions! So, use this space to design your day.

Write what you'd love to happen each day, then visualise it, manifest it, action it and make it happen.

WHY YOUR ACTIONS MATTER SO MUCH

"Vision without action is nothing. It's one thing to have a big dream, but it's another to actually action it." Our opening quote really captures why creating and designing your actionable steps is so damn important.

You can be a dreamer, a "gonna-doer", "I'll do it tomorrow" or "I'll do this when ..." kind of person. *Or* you can be a visualiser *and* actioner, and work your butt off to create your dreams by any means necessary.

So, actions are just as important as visions.

Remember to note down your actionable strategies for each of your goals in your Daily Accountability planner, and track those you achieve and those you don't.

For whatever you don't achieve, consider the reasons. Then, list it again for the next day and come up with a new actionable plan to *make it happen*!

questionnaire

QUICK QUESTIONS TO KICK OFF!

A good way to get started practising visualising and actioning is to reflect on your life so far. Think about the biggest and best moments.
Think about your achievements and moments when you smashed your goals. You probably felt 'in flow', and that somehow things were easier than usual.

There was a certain almost unexplained synchronicity and serendipity and things just started to unfold in the most perfect of ways. If you think back to the vision and actions you took prior to these things seemingly miraculously unfolding, you may find yourself nodding a little retrospective, "Aha! I see what I did there."

Answer the following questions to bring attention to these moments, rediscover and reverse engineer what steps you took to succeed. Take time when answering each question and really try to relive your answers as you're writing. Be in the moment and enjoy your trip down memory lane!

What was your biggest achievement from your early childhood?

_____

_____

_____

_____

How did you achieve this?

_____

_____

_____

_____

_____

_____

_____

What was your biggest achievement as a teenager?

___

___

___

___

How did you achieve this?

___

___

___

___

___

___

___

___

What has been the biggest achievement in your career so far?

___

___

___

___

How did you achieve this?

___

___

___

___

___

___

___

___

What has been your biggest achievement in health, fitness and wellbeing?

___

___

___

___

How did you achieve this?

___

___

___

___

___

___

___

___

DAILY ACCOUNTABILITY

Today's mantra: I will consume less and make better choices.

Date: ___ / ___ / _____

Today, I am feeling:

- EXCITED
- STRESSED
- ENERGETIC
- HAPPY
- RELAXED
- RESTED
- SLEEPY
- APATHETIC
- SAD

Daily visualisation

In life: _____

In career: _____

In health/wellness: _____

The BIG goal I'm working towards today:

Today's priorities:

Top three mini goals:

1. _____

2. _____

3. _____

Reflection:

Today's three biggest wins:

1. _____

2. _____

3. _____

DAILY ACCOUNTABILITY

Today's mantra: I am strong, i am resiliant.

Date: ___ /___ /____

Today, I am feeling:

- EXCITED
- STRESSED
- ENERGETIC
- HAPPY
- RELAXED
- RESTED
- SLEEPY
- APATHETIC
- SAD

Daily visualisation

In life: _____

In career: _____

In health/wellness: _____

> The BIG goal I'm working towards today:

Today's priorities:

Top three mini goals:

1. _____

2. _____

3. _____

Reflection:

Today's three biggest wins:

1. _____

2. _____

3. _____

VISIONS & ACTIONS

WEEKLY RECAP

"There's a lot of power in sending positive vibes to those around you."
@collectivehub

Did I complete the past seven days?   Yes ☐   No ☐

If no, why did I miss the day/days: _____

_____

I can do better next week by: _____

_____

My best and/or biggest achievement of the week was:

_____

How is my progress is going towards your big goal?

_____

Reflection:

Some visualisation tools I used this week:

1. _____

2. _____

3. _____

My big actions for next week:

Rate your week: ___ / 10

DAILY ACCOUNTABILITY

Today's mantra: I will show those around me that i love them.

Date: ___ /___ /_____

Today, I am feeling:

- EXCITED
- STRESSED
- ENERGETIC

- HAPPY
- RELAXED
- RESTED

- SLEEPY
- APATHETIC
- SAD

Daily visualisation

In life: _____

In career: _____

In health/wellness: _____

The BIG goal I'm working towards today:

Today's priorities:

Top three mini goals:

1. _____

2. _____

3. _____

Reflection:

Today's three biggest wins:

1. _____

2. _____

3. _____

DAILY ACCOUNTABILITY

Today's mantra: I will live each moment in the present.

Date: ___ /___ /_____

Today, I am feeling:

- EXCITED
- STRESSED
- ENERGETIC

- HAPPY
- RELAXED
- RESTED

- SLEEPY
- APATHETIC
- SAD

Daily visualisation

In life: _____

In career: _____

In health/wellness: _____

The BIG goal I'm working towards today:

Today's priorities:

Top three mini goals:

1. _____

2. _____

3. _____

Reflection:

Today's three biggest wins:

1. _____

2. _____

3. _____

JOURNALING

DAILY ACCOUNTABILITY

Today's mantra: I will fuel my mind with positivity.

Date: ___ / ___ / _____

Today, I am feeling:

- EXCITED
- STRESSED
- ENERGETIC
- HAPPY
- RELAXED
- RESTED
- SLEEPY
- APATHETIC
- SAD

Daily visualisation

In life: _____

In career: _____

In health/wellness: _____

The BIG goal I'm working towards today:

Today's priorities:

Top three mini goals:

1. _____

2. _____

3. _____

Reflection:

Today's three biggest wins:

1. _____

2. _____

3. _____

DAILY ACCOUNTABILITY

Today's mantra: I will not let others' opinions affect how i live my life.

Date: ___ /___ /____

Today, I am feeling:

- EXCITED
- STRESSED
- ENERGETIC
- HAPPY
- RELAXED
- RESTED
- SLEEPY
- APATHETIC
- SAD

Daily visualisation

In life: _____

In career: _____

In health/wellness: _____

The BIG goal I'm working towards today:

Today's priorities:

Top three mini goals:

1. _____

2. _____

3. _____

Reflection:

Today's three biggest wins:

1. _____

2. _____

3. _____

DAILY ACCOUNTABILITY

Today's mantra: I am loved.

Date: ___ /___ /_____

Today, I am feeling:

- EXCITED
- STRESSED
- ENERGETIC
- HAPPY
- RELAXED
- RESTED
- SLEEPY
- APATHETIC
- SAD

Daily visualisation

In life: _____

In career: _____

In health/wellness: _____

The BIG goal I'm working towards today:

Today's priorities:

Top three mini goals:

1. _____

2. _____

3. _____

Reflection:

Today's three biggest wins:

1. _____

2. _____

3. _____

DAILY ACCOUNTABILITY

Today's mantra: I choose to live selflessly.

Date: ___ /___ /_____

Today, I am feeling:

- EXCITED
- STRESSED
- ENERGETIC
- HAPPY
- RELAXED
- RESTED
- SLEEPY
- APATHETIC
- SAD

Daily visualisation

In life: _____

In career: _____

In health/wellness: _____

The BIG goal I'm working towards today:

Today's priorities:

Top three mini goals:

1. _____

2. _____

3. _____

Reflection:

Today's three biggest wins:

1. _____

2. _____

3. _____

JOURNALING

DAILY ACCOUNTABILITY

Today's mantra: I will choose my people and places wisely.

Date: ___ / ___ / _____

Today, I am feeling:

- EXCITED
- STRESSED
- ENERGETIC
- HAPPY
- RELAXED
- RESTED
- SLEEPY
- APATHETIC
- SAD

Daily visualisation

In life: _____

In career: _____

In health/wellness: _____

The BIG goal I'm working towards today:

Today's priorities:

Top three mini goals:

1. _____

2. _____

3. _____

Reflection:

Today's three biggest wins:

1. _____

2. _____

3. _____

WEEKLY RECAP

*"Be yourself. People don't have to like you.
And you don't have to care."*

– Anon

Did I complete the past seven days?   Yes ☐   No ☐

If no, why did I miss the day/days: _____

_____

I can do better next week by: _____

_____

My best and/or biggest achievement of the week was:

_____

How is my progress is going towards your big goal?

_____

Reflection:

Some visualisation tools I used this week:

1. _____

2. _____

3. _____

My big actions for next week:

Rate your week: / 10

DAILY ACCOUNTABILITY

Today's mantra: I am eager to explore new adventures.

Date: ___ /___ /_____

Today, I am feeling:

- EXCITED
- STRESSED
- ENERGETIC
- HAPPY
- RELAXED
- RESTED
- SLEEPY
- APATHETIC
- SAD

Daily visualisation

In life: _____

In career: _____

In health/wellness: _____

The BIG goal I'm working towards today:

Today's priorities:

Top three mini goals:

1. _____

2. _____

3. _____

Reflection:

Today's three biggest wins:

1. _____

2. _____

3. _____

DAILY ACCOUNTABILITY

Today's mantra: I am creating a life that is full of purpose.

Date: ___ /___ /____

Today, I am feeling:

- EXCITED
- HAPPY
- SLEEPY
- STRESSED
- RELAXED
- APATHETIC
- ENERGETIC
- RESTED
- SAD

Daily visualisation

In life: _____

In career: _____

In health/wellness: _____

The BIG goal I'm working towards today:

Today's priorities:

Top three mini goals:

1. _____

2. _____

3. _____

Reflection:

Today's three biggest wins:

1. _____

2. _____

3. _____

DAILY ACCOUNTABILITY

Today's mantra: I choose to live my life authentically.

Date: ___ / ___ / _____

Today, I am feeling:

- EXCITED
- STRESSED
- ENERGETIC
- HAPPY
- RELAXED
- RESTED
- SLEEPY
- APATHETIC
- SAD

Daily visualisation

In life: _____

In career: _____

In health/wellness: _____

The BIG goal I'm working towards today:

Today's priorities:

Top three mini goals:

1. _____

2. _____

3. _____

Reflection:

Today's three biggest wins:

1. _____

2. _____

3. _____

DAILY ACCOUNTABILITY

Today's mantra: I will be open-minded.

Date: ___ / ___ / _____

Today, I am feeling:

- EXCITED
- STRESSED
- ENERGETIC
- HAPPY
- RELAXED
- RESTED
- SLEEPY
- APATHETIC
- SAD

Daily visualisation

In life: _____

In career: _____

In health/wellness: _____

The BIG goal I'm working towards today:

Today's priorities:

Top three mini goals:

1. _____

2. _____

3. _____

Reflection:

Today's three biggest wins:

1. _____

2. _____

3. _____

DAILY ACCOUNTABILITY

Today's mantra: I am enthusiastic and passionate about my desires.

Date: ___ / ___ / _____

Today, I am feeling:

- EXCITED
- STRESSED
- ENERGETIC
- HAPPY
- RELAXED
- RESTED
- SLEEPY
- APATHETIC
- SAD

Daily visualisation

In life: _____

In career: _____

In health/wellness: _____

The BIG goal I'm working towards today:

Today's priorities:

Top three mini goals:

1. _____

2. _____

3. _____

Reflection:

Today's three biggest wins:

1. _____

2. _____

3. _____

DAILY ACCOUNTABILITY

Today's mantra: I am the architect of my life.

Date: ___ /___ /_____

Today, I am feeling:

- EXCITED
- STRESSED
- ENERGETIC
- HAPPY
- RELAXED
- RESTED
- SLEEPY
- APATHETIC
- SAD

Daily visualisation

In life: _____

In career: _____

In health/wellness: _____

```
The BIG goal I'm working towards today:



```

Today's priorities:

Top three mini goals:

1. _____

2. _____

3. _____

Reflection:

Today's three biggest wins:

1. _____

2. _____

3. _____

DAILY ACCOUNTABILITY

Today's mantra: I am never alone.

Date: ___ /___ /____

Today, I am feeling:

- EXCITED
- STRESSED
- ENERGETIC
- HAPPY
- RELAXED
- RESTED
- SLEEPY
- APATHETIC
- SAD

Daily visualisation

In life: _____

In career: _____

In health/wellness: _____

The BIG goal I'm working towards today:

Today's priorities:

Top three mini goals:

1. _____

2. _____

3. _____

Reflection:

Today's three biggest wins:

1. _____

2. _____

3. _____

WEEKLY RECAP

"Only put out what you want back."

@collectivehub

Did I complete the past seven days?   Yes ☐   No ☐

If no, why did I miss the day/days: _____

_____

I can do better next week by: _____

_____

My best and/or biggest achievement of the week was:

_____

How is my progress is going towards your big goal?

_____

Reflection:

Some visualisation tools I used this week:

1. _____

2. _____

3. _____

My big actions for next week:

Rate your week: /10

DAILY ACCOUNTABILITY

Today's mantra: I choose to think positively.

Date: ___ / ___ / _____

Today, I am feeling:

- EXCITED
- STRESSED
- ENERGETIC
- HAPPY
- RELAXED
- RESTED
- SLEEPY
- APATHETIC
- SAD

Daily visualisation

In life: _____

In career: _____

In health/wellness: _____

The BIG goal I'm working towards today:

Today's priorities:

Top three mini goals:

1. _____

2. _____

3. _____

Reflection:

Today's three biggest wins:

1. _____

2. _____

3. _____

DAILY ACCOUNTABILITY

Today's mantra: I will lead a wonderful and successful life.

Date: ___ /___ /_____

Today, I am feeling:

- EXCITED
- STRESSED
- ENERGETIC
- HAPPY
- RELAXED
- RESTED
- SLEEPY
- APATHETIC
- SAD

Daily visualisation

In life: _____

In career: _____

In health/wellness: _____

The BIG goal I'm working towards today:

Today's priorities:

Top three mini goals:

1. _____

2. _____

3. _____

Reflection:

Today's three biggest wins:

1. _____

2. _____

3. _____

DAILY ACCOUNTABILITY

Today's mantra: I have the power to create happiness.

Date: ___ /___ /_____

Today, I am feeling:

- EXCITED
- STRESSED
- ENERGETIC
- HAPPY
- RELAXED
- RESTED
- SLEEPY
- APATHETIC
- SAD

Daily visualisation

In life: _____

In career: _____

In health/wellness: _____

> The BIG goal I'm working towards today:

Today's priorities:

Top three mini goals:

1. _____

2. _____

3. _____

Reflection:

Today's three biggest wins:

1. _____

2. _____

3. _____

DAILY ACCOUNTABILITY

Today's mantra: What exactly am I racing towards?

Date: ___ / ___ / _____

Today, I am feeling:

- EXCITED
- STRESSED
- ENERGETIC
- HAPPY
- RELAXED
- RESTED
- SLEEPY
- APATHETIC
- SAD

Daily visualisation

In life: _____

In career: _____

In health/wellness: _____

```
The BIG goal I'm working towards today:



```

Today's priorities:

Top three mini goals:

1. _____

2. _____

3. _____

Reflection:

Today's three biggest wins:

1. _____

2. _____

3. _____

DAILY ACCOUNTABILITY

Today's mantra: I will achieve my results by staying accountable.

Date: ___ /___ /_____

Today, I am feeling:

- EXCITED
- STRESSED
- ENERGETIC
- HAPPY
- RELAXED
- RESTED
- SLEEPY
- APATHETIC
- SAD

Daily visualisation

In life: _____

In career: _____

In health/wellness: _____

The BIG goal I'm working towards today:

Today's priorities:

Top three mini goals:

1. _____

2. _____

3. _____

Reflection:

Today's three biggest wins:

1. _____

2. _____

3. _____

DAILY ACCOUNTABILITY

Today's mantra: I have no doubts.

Date: ___ /___ /_____

Today, I am feeling:

- EXCITED
- STRESSED
- ENERGETIC
- HAPPY
- RELAXED
- RESTED
- SLEEPY
- APATHETIC
- SAD

Daily visualisation

In life: _____

In career: _____

In health/wellness: _____

> The BIG goal I'm working towards today:

Today's priorities:

Top three mini goals:

1. _____

2. _____

3. _____

Reflection:

Today's three biggest wins:

1. _____

2. _____

3. _____

DAILY ACCOUNTABILITY

Today's mantra: I am enough on my own.

Date: ___ / ___ / _____

Today, I am feeling:

- EXCITED
- STRESSED
- ENERGETIC
- HAPPY
- RELAXED
- RESTED
- SLEEPY
- APATHETIC
- SAD

Daily visualisation

In life: _____

In career: _____

In health/wellness: _____

The BIG goal I'm working towards today:

Today's priorities:

Top three mini goals:

1. _____

2. _____

3. _____

Reflection:

Today's three biggest wins:

1. _____

2. _____

3. _____

WEEKLY RECAP

*"Sometimes you will never know the value
of a moment until it becomes a memory."*

– Dr Seuss

Did I complete the past seven days?   Yes ☐   No ☐

If no, why did I miss the day/days: _____

_____

I can do better next week by: _____

_____

My best and/or biggest achievement of the week was:

_____

How is my progress is going towards your big goal?

_____

Reflection:

Some visualisation tools I used this week:

1. _____

2. _____

3. _____

My big actions for next week:

Rate your week: ⎯⎯ /10

monthly review

"Sometimes, the very thing that you're afraid of doing is the precise thing that will allow you to be free."

@lisamessenger

The single biggest/best achievement for the month was:

___

I'm most proud of:

___

My best visualisation strategy was:

___

Three things I loved about this month:

1. _____
2. _____
3. _____

My healthiest action was:

My best career move/decision was:

My best mindset practice was:

I felt most successful/enlightened when:

The best moment of courage I had:

A visualisation that came true was:

Three things that didn't go to plan this month:

1. _____
2. _____
3. _____

How I can avoid or improve these things next month:

1. _____
2. _____
3. _____

Three visions and actions I undertook and achieved this month:

1. _____
2. _____
3. _____

> **Don't fear failure so much that you refuse to try new things. The saddest summary of a life contains three descriptions:**

could have, might have, and should have.
"

– Louis E Boone

DAILY ACCOUNTABILITY

Today's mantra: My health is my wealth.

Date: ___ / ___ / _____

Today, I am feeling:

- EXCITED
- STRESSED
- ENERGETIC
- HAPPY
- RELAXED
- RESTED
- SLEEPY
- APATHETIC
- SAD

Daily visualisation

In life: _____

In career: _____

In health/wellness: _____

The BIG goal I'm working towards today:

Today's priorities:

Top three mini goals:

1. _____

2. _____

3. _____

Reflection:

Today's three biggest wins:

1. _____

2. _____

3. _____

DAILY ACCOUNTABILITY

Today's mantra: I will seek soulful connections.

Date: ___ / ___ / _____

Today, I am feeling:

- EXCITED
- HAPPY
- SLEEPY
- STRESSED
- RELAXED
- APATHETIC
- ENERGETIC
- RESTED
- SAD

Daily visualisation

In life: _____

In career: _____

In health/wellness: _____

The BIG goal I'm working towards today:

Today's priorities:

Top three mini goals:

1. _____

2. _____

3. _____

Reflection:

Today's three biggest wins:

1. _____

2. _____

3. _____

DAILY ACCOUNTABILITY

Today's mantra: I am the master of my destiny.

Date: ___ /___ /_____

Today, I am feeling:

- EXCITED
- STRESSED
- ENERGETIC
- HAPPY
- RELAXED
- RESTED
- SLEEPY
- APATHETIC
- SAD

Daily visualisation

In life: _____

In career: _____

In health/wellness: _____

The BIG goal I'm working towards today:

Today's priorities:

Top three mini goals:

1. _____

2. _____

3. _____

Reflection:

Today's three biggest wins:

1. _____

2. _____

3. _____

DAILY ACCOUNTABILITY

Today's mantra: I will cherish my loved ones.

Date: ___ /___ /_____

Today, I am feeling:

- EXCITED
- HAPPY
- SLEEPY
- STRESSED
- RELAXED
- APATHETIC
- ENERGETIC
- RESTED
- SAD

Daily visualisation

In life: _____

In career: _____

In health/wellness: _____

The BIG goal I'm working towards today:

Today's priorities:

Top three mini goals:

1. _____

2. _____

3. _____

Reflection:

Today's three biggest wins:

1. _____

2. _____

3. _____

DAILY ACCOUNTABILITY

Today's mantra: I am powerful.

Date: ___ / ___ / _____

Today, I am feeling:

- EXCITED
- STRESSED
- ENERGETIC
- HAPPY
- RELAXED
- RESTED
- SLEEPY
- APATHETIC
- SAD

Daily visualisation

In life: _____

In career: _____

In health/wellness: _____

> The BIG goal I'm working towards today:

Today's priorities:

Top three mini goals:

1. _____

2. _____

3. _____

Reflection:

Today's three biggest wins:

1. _____

2. _____

3. _____

DAILY ACCOUNTABILITY

Today's mantra: I create the life I want.

Date: ___ /___ /_____

Today, I am feeling:

- EXCITED
- STRESSED
- ENERGETIC
- HAPPY
- RELAXED
- RESTED
- SLEEPY
- APATHETIC
- SAD

Daily visualisation

In life: _____

In career: _____

In health/wellness: _____

The BIG goal I'm working towards today:

Today's priorities:

Top three mini goals:

1. _____

2. _____

3. _____

Reflection:

Today's three biggest wins:

1. _____

2. _____

3. _____

DAILY ACCOUNTABILITY

Today's mantra: My confidence is rising.

Date: ___ /___ /_____

Today, I am feeling:

- EXCITED
- STRESSED
- ENERGETIC
- HAPPY
- RELAXED
- RESTED
- SLEEPY
- APATHETIC
- SAD

Daily visualisation

In life: _____

In career: _____

In health/wellness: _____

The BIG goal I'm working towards today:

Today's priorities:

Top three mini goals:

1. _____

2. _____

3. _____

Reflection:

Today's three biggest wins:

1. _____

2. _____

3. _____

WEEKLY RECAP

*"Ten years from now, make sure you can say that
you chose your life, you didn't settle for it."*

– Mandy Hale

Did I complete the past seven days?   Yes ☐   No ☐

If no, why did I miss the day/days: _____

_____

I can do better next week by: _____

_____

My best and/or biggest achievement of the week was:

_____

How is my progress is going towards your big goal?

_____

Reflection:

Some visualisation tools I used this week:

1. _____

2. _____

3. _____

My big actions for next week:

Rate your week: ___ / 10

DAILY ACCOUNTABILITY

Today's mantra: I will allow gratitude to fill my life.

Date: ___ / ___ / _____

Today, I am feeling:

- EXCITED
- STRESSED
- ENERGETIC
- HAPPY
- RELAXED
- RESTED
- SLEEPY
- APATHETIC
- SAD

Daily visualisation

In life: _____

In career: _____

In health/wellness: _____

The BIG goal I'm working towards today:

Today's priorities:

Top three mini goals:

1. _____

2. _____

3. _____

Reflection:

Today's three biggest wins:

1. _____

2. _____

3. _____

DAILY ACCOUNTABILITY

Today's mantra: Happiness is all around me.

Date: ___ /___ /_____

Today, I am feeling:

- EXCITED
- STRESSED
- ENERGETIC
- HAPPY
- RELAXED
- RESTED
- SLEEPY
- APATHETIC
- SAD

Daily visualisation

In life: _____

In career: _____

In health/wellness: _____

The BIG goal I'm working towards today:

Today's priorities:

Top three mini goals:

1. _____

2. _____

3. _____

Reflection:

Today's three biggest wins:

1. _____

2. _____

3. _____

DAILY ACCOUNTABILITY

Today's mantra: I will push forward, no matter what.

Date: ___ /___ /_____

Today, I am feeling:

- EXCITED
- STRESSED
- ENERGETIC
- HAPPY
- RELAXED
- RESTED
- SLEEPY
- APATHETIC
- SAD

Daily visualisation

In life: _____

In career: _____

In health/wellness: _____

> The BIG goal I'm working towards today:

Today's priorities:

Top three mini goals:

1. _____

2. _____

3. _____

Reflection:

Today's three biggest wins:

1. _____

2. _____

3. _____

DAILY ACCOUNTABILITY

Today's mantra: I will succeed today.

Date: ___ /___ /_____

Today, I am feeling:

- EXCITED
- STRESSED
- ENERGETIC
- HAPPY
- RELAXED
- RESTED
- SLEEPY
- APATHETIC
- SAD

Daily visualisation

In life: _____

In career: _____

In health/wellness: _____

The BIG goal I'm working towards today:

Today's priorities:

Top three mini goals:

1. _____

2. _____

3. _____

Reflection:

Today's three biggest wins:

1. _____

2. _____

3. _____

DAILY ACCOUNTABILITY

Today's mantra: I will help those around me.

Date: ___ / ___ / ____

Today, I am feeling:

- EXCITED
- STRESSED
- ENERGETIC
- HAPPY
- RELAXED
- RESTED
- SLEEPY
- APATHETIC
- SAD

Daily visualisation

In life: _____

In career: _____

In health/wellness: _____

The BIG goal I'm working towards today:

Today's priorities:

Top three mini goals:

1. _____

2. _____

3. _____

Reflection:

Today's three biggest wins:

1. _____

2. _____

3. _____

DAILY ACCOUNTABILITY

Today's mantra: I have all that I need to make today great.

Date: ___ / ___ / _____

Today, I am feeling:

- EXCITED
- STRESSED
- ENERGETIC
- HAPPY
- RELAXED
- RESTED
- SLEEPY
- APATHETIC
- SAD

Daily visualisation

In life: _____

In career: _____

In health/wellness: _____

The BIG goal I'm working towards today:

Today's priorities:

Top three mini goals:

1. _____

2. _____

3. _____

Reflection:

Today's three biggest wins:

1. _____

2. _____

3. _____

DAILY ACCOUNTABILITY

Today's mantra: I am ready for change.

Date: ___ /___ /_____

Today, I am feeling:

- EXCITED
- STRESSED
- ENERGETIC
- HAPPY
- RELAXED
- RESTED
- SLEEPY
- APATHETIC
- SAD

Daily visualisation

In life: _____

In career: _____

In health/wellness: _____

The BIG goal I'm working towards today:

Today's priorities:

Top three mini goals:

1. _____

2. _____

3. _____

Reflection:

Today's three biggest wins:

1. _____

2. _____

3. _____

WEEKLY RECAP

"Your limitation — it's only your imagination."

– Anon

Did I complete the past seven days?   Yes ☐   No ☐

If no, why did I miss the day/days: _____

_____

I can do better next week by: _____

_____

My best and/or biggest achievement of the week was:

_____

How is my progress is going towards your big goal?

_____

Reflection:

Some visualisation tools I used this week:

1. _____

2. _____

3. _____

My big actions for next week:

Rate your week: / 10

DAILY ACCOUNTABILITY

Today's mantra: I am passionate about my goals.

Date: ___ / ___ / _____

Today, I am feeling:

- EXCITED
- STRESSED
- ENERGETIC
- HAPPY
- RELAXED
- RESTED
- SLEEPY
- APATHETIC
- SAD

Daily visualisation

In life: _____

In career: _____

In health/wellness: _____

The BIG goal I'm working towards today:

Today's priorities:

Top three mini goals:

1. _____

2. _____

3. _____

Reflection:

Today's three biggest wins:

1. _____

2. _____

3. _____

DAILY ACCOUNTABILITY

Today's mantra: I am courageous.

Date: ___ / ___ / _____

Today, I am feeling:

- EXCITED
- STRESSED
- ENERGETIC
- HAPPY
- RELAXED
- RESTED
- SLEEPY
- APATHETIC
- SAD

Daily visualisation

In life: _____

In career: _____

In health/wellness: _____

The BIG goal I'm working towards today:

Today's priorities:

Top three mini goals:

1. _____

2. _____

3. _____

Reflection:

Today's three biggest wins:

1. _____

2. _____

3. _____

DAILY ACCOUNTABILITY

Today's mantra: I will face my fears.

Date: ___ /___ /_____

Today, I am feeling:

- EXCITED
- STRESSED
- ENERGETIC
- HAPPY
- RELAXED
- RESTED
- SLEEPY
- APATHETIC
- SAD

Daily visualisation

In life: _____

In career: _____

In health/wellness: _____

The BIG goal I'm working towards today:

Today's priorities:

Top three mini goals:

1. _____

2. _____

3. _____

Reflection:

Today's three biggest wins:

1. _____

2. _____

3. _____

DAILY ACCOUNTABILITY

Today's mantra: I am powerful in my vulnerability.

Date: ___ /___ /_____

Today, I am feeling:

- EXCITED
- STRESSED
- ENERGETIC
- HAPPY
- RELAXED
- RESTED
- SLEEPY
- APATHETIC
- SAD

Daily visualisation

In life: _____

In career: _____

In health/wellness: _____

The BIG goal I'm working towards today:

Today's priorities:

Top three mini goals:

1. _____

2. _____

3. _____

Reflection:

Today's three biggest wins:

1. _____

2. _____

3. _____

DAILY ACCOUNTABILITY

Today's mantra: I am always on a quest to better myself.

Date: ___ / ___ / _____

Today, I am feeling:

- EXCITED
- STRESSED
- ENERGETIC
- HAPPY
- RELAXED
- RESTED
- SLEEPY
- APATHETIC
- SAD

Daily visualisation

In life: _____

In career: _____

In health/wellness: _____

The BIG goal I'm working towards today:

Today's priorities:

Top three mini goals:

1. _____

2. _____

3. _____

Reflection:

Today's three biggest wins:

1. _____

2. _____

3. _____

DAILY ACCOUNTABILITY

Today's mantra: I believe in my strength.

Date: ___ /___ /_____

Today, I am feeling:

- EXCITED
- STRESSED
- ENERGETIC
- HAPPY
- RELAXED
- RESTED
- SLEEPY
- APATHETIC
- SAD

Daily visualisation

In life: _____

In career: _____

In health/wellness: _____

The BIG goal I'm working towards today:

Today's priorities:

Top three mini goals:

1. _____

2. _____

3. _____

Reflection:

Today's three biggest wins:

1. _____

2. _____

3. _____

DAILY ACCOUNTABILITY

Today's mantra: I will overcome obstacles and adversities.

Date: ___ /___ /____

Today, I am feeling:

- EXCITED
- STRESSED
- ENERGETIC
- HAPPY
- RELAXED
- RESTED
- SLEEPY
- APATHETIC
- SAD

Daily visualisation

In life: _____

In career: _____

In health/wellness: _____

The BIG goal I'm working towards today:

Today's priorities:

Top three mini goals:

1. _____

2. _____

3. _____

Reflection:

Today's three biggest wins:

1. _____

2. _____

3. _____

WEEKLY RECAP

"Courage doesn't always roar. Sometimes courage is the little voice at the end of the day that says I'll try again tomorrow."

– Mary Anne Radmacher

Did I complete the past seven days?   Yes ☐   No ☐

If no, why did I miss the day/days: _____

_____

I can do better next week by: _____

_____

My best and/or biggest achievement of the week was:

_____

How is my progress is going towards your big goal?

_____

Reflection:

Some visualisation tools I used this week:

1. _____

2. _____

3. _____

Rate your week: ___ / 10

My big actions for next week:

DAILY ACCOUNTABILITY

Today's mantra: My actions are intentional.

Date: ___ / ___ / _____

Today, I am feeling:

- EXCITED
- STRESSED
- ENERGETIC
- HAPPY
- RELAXED
- RESTED
- SLEEPY
- APATHETIC
- SAD

Daily visualisation

In life: _____

In career: _____

In health/wellness: _____

The BIG goal I'm working towards today:

Today's priorities:

Top three mini goals:

1. _____

2. _____

3. _____

Reflection:

Today's three biggest wins:

1. _____

2. _____

3. _____

DAILY ACCOUNTABILITY

Today's mantra: I am happy and free because I am me.

Date: ___ /___ /_____

Today, I am feeling:

- EXCITED
- STRESSED
- ENERGETIC
- HAPPY
- RELAXED
- RESTED
- SLEEPY
- APATHETIC
- SAD

Daily visualisation

In life: _____

In career: _____

In health/wellness: _____

> The BIG goal I'm working towards today:

Today's priorities:

Top three mini goals:

1. _____

2. _____

3. _____

Reflection:

Today's three biggest wins:

1. _____

2. _____

3. _____

DAILY ACCOUNTABILITY

Today's mantra: I am surrounded by supportive and positive people.

Date: ___ /___ /_____

Today, I am feeling:

- EXCITED
- STRESSED
- ENERGETIC
- HAPPY
- RELAXED
- RESTED
- SLEEPY
- APATHETIC
- SAD

Daily visualisation

In life: _____

In career: _____

In health/wellness: _____

The BIG goal I'm working towards today:

Today's priorities:

Top three mini goals:

1. _____

2. _____

3. _____

Reflection:

Today's three biggest wins:

1. _____

2. _____

3. _____

DAILY ACCOUNTABILITY

Today's mantra: I believe in me.

Date: ___ /___ /_____

Today, I am feeling:

- EXCITED
- STRESSED
- ENERGETIC
- HAPPY
- RELAXED
- RESTED
- SLEEPY
- APATHETIC
- SAD

Daily visualisation

In life: _____

In career: _____

In health/wellness: _____

The BIG goal I'm working towards today:

Today's priorities:

Top three mini goals:

1. _____

2. _____

3. _____

Reflection:

Today's three biggest wins:

1. _____

2. _____

3. _____

DAILY ACCOUNTABILITY

Today's mantra: I am grateful for everyday happiness.

Date: ___ /___ /_____

Today, I am feeling:

- EXCITED
- STRESSED
- ENERGETIC
- HAPPY
- RELAXED
- RESTED
- SLEEPY
- APATHETIC
- SAD

Daily visualisation

In life: _____

In career: _____

In health/wellness: _____

The BIG goal I'm working towards today:

Today's priorities:

Top three mini goals:

1. _____

2. _____

3. _____

Reflection:

Today's three biggest wins:

1. _____

2. _____

3. _____

DAILY ACCOUNTABILITY

Today's mantra: I will celebrate today with gratitude and joy.

Date: ___ /___ /_____

Today, I am feeling:

- EXCITED
- STRESSED
- ENERGETIC
- HAPPY
- RELAXED
- RESTED
- SLEEPY
- APATHETIC
- SAD

Daily visualisation

In life: _____

In career: _____

In health/wellness: _____

The BIG goal I'm working towards today:

Today's priorities:

Top three mini goals:

1. _____

2. _____

3. _____

Reflection:

Today's three biggest wins:

1. _____

2. _____

3. _____

DAILY ACCOUNTABILITY

Today's mantra: I will let go of the old and welcome the new.

Date: ___ / ___ / _____

Today, I am feeling:

- EXCITED
- STRESSED
- ENERGETIC
- HAPPY
- RELAXED
- RESTED
- SLEEPY
- APATHETIC
- SAD

Daily visualisation

In life: _____

In career: _____

In health/wellness: _____

The BIG goal I'm working towards today:

Today's priorities:

Top three mini goals:

1. _____

2. _____

3. _____

Reflection:

Today's three biggest wins:

1. _____

2. _____

3. _____

WEEKLY RECAP

"Maybe we're just stars colliding — that's why people come and go."

– Anon

Did I complete the past seven days?   Yes ☐   No ☐

If no, why did I miss the day/days: _____

_____

I can do better next week by: _____

_____

My best and/or biggest achievement of the week was:

_____

How is my progress is going towards your big goal?

_____

Reflection:

Some visualisation tools I used this week:

1. _____

2. _____

3. _____

My big actions for next week:

Rate your week: /10

monthly review

"Every next level of your life will demand a different version of you."

– Leonardo DiCaprio

The single biggest/best achievement for the month was:
_____
_____
_____
_____

I'm most proud of:
_____
_____
_____
_____

My best visualisation strategy was:
_____
_____
_____
_____
_____

Three things I loved about this month:

1. _____
2. _____
3. _____

My healthiest action was:

My best career move/decision was:

My best mindset practice was:

I felt most successful/enlightened when:

The best moment of courage I had:

A visualisation that came true was:

Three things that didn't go to plan this month:

1. _____
2. _____
3. _____

How I can avoid or improve these things next month:

1. _____
2. _____
3. _____

Three visions and actions I undertook and achieved this month:

1. _____
2. _____
3. _____

"
And in the end, of all the things I wish to say about my life, most importantly I want to be able to say

> **I was doing life the best I knew how and learning continuously to do it better.**

Rebecca Ray

DAILY ACCOUNTABILITY

Today's mantra: I am stronger and wiser for staying uniquely me.

Date: ___ / ___ / ____

Today, I am feeling:

- EXCITED
- STRESSED
- ENERGETIC
- HAPPY
- RELAXED
- RESTED
- SLEEPY
- APATHETIC
- SAD

Daily visualisation

In life: _____

In career: _____

In health/wellness: _____

The BIG goal I'm working towards today:

Today's priorities:

Top three mini goals:

1. _____

2. _____

3. _____

Reflection:

Today's three biggest wins:

1. _____

2. _____

3. _____

DAILY ACCOUNTABILITY

Today's mantra: I breathe happy thoughts in and sad thoughts out.

Date: ___ /___ /_____

Today, I am feeling:

- EXCITED
- STRESSED
- ENERGETIC
- HAPPY
- RELAXED
- RESTED
- SLEEPY
- APATHETIC
- SAD

Daily visualisation

In life: _____

In career: _____

In health/wellness: _____

The BIG goal I'm working towards today:

Today's priorities:

Top three mini goals:

1. _____

2. _____

3. _____

Reflection:

Today's three biggest wins:

1. _____

2. _____

3. _____

DAILY ACCOUNTABILITY

Today's mantra: I am present and full of love.

Date: ___ / ___ / _____

Today, I am feeling:

- EXCITED
- STRESSED
- ENERGETIC
- HAPPY
- RELAXED
- RESTED
- SLEEPY
- APATHETIC
- SAD

Daily visualisation

In life: _____

In career: _____

In health/wellness: _____

The BIG goal I'm working towards today:

Today's priorities:

Top three mini goals:

1. _____

2. _____

3. _____

Reflection:

Today's three biggest wins:

1. _____

2. _____

3. _____

DAILY ACCOUNTABILITY

Today's mantra: I can overcome whatever life throws at me.

Date: ___ /___ /_____

Today, I am feeling:

- EXCITED
- STRESSED
- ENERGETIC
- HAPPY
- RELAXED
- RESTED
- SLEEPY
- APATHETIC
- SAD

Daily visualisation

In life: _____

In career: _____

In health/wellness: _____

The BIG goal I'm working towards today:

Today's priorities:

Top three mini goals:

1. _____

2. _____

3. _____

Reflection:

Today's three biggest wins:

1. _____

2. _____

3. _____

DAILY ACCOUNTABILITY

Today's mantra: I will practise being softer and kinder.

Date: ___ /___ /____

Today, I am feeling:

- EXCITED
- STRESSED
- ENERGETIC
- HAPPY
- RELAXED
- RESTED
- SLEEPY
- APATHETIC
- SAD

Daily visualisation

In life: _____

In career: _____

In health/wellness: _____

The BIG goal I'm working towards today:

Today's priorities:

Top three mini goals:

1. _____

2. _____

3. _____

Reflection:

Today's three biggest wins:

1. _____

2. _____

3. _____

DAILY ACCOUNTABILITY

Today's mantra: I respect those around me.

Date: ___ / ___ / _____

Today, I am feeling:

- EXCITED
- HAPPY
- SLEEPY
- STRESSED
- RELAXED
- APATHETIC
- ENERGETIC
- RESTED
- SAD

Daily visualisation

In life: _____

In career: _____

In health/wellness: _____

> The BIG goal I'm working towards today:

Today's priorities:

Top three mini goals:

1. _____

2. _____

3. _____

Reflection:

Today's three biggest wins:

1. _____

2. _____

3. _____

DAILY ACCOUNTABILITY

Today's mantra: I am thankful for the small things today will bring.

Date: ___ / ___ / _____

Today, I am feeling:

- EXCITED
- STRESSED
- ENERGETIC
- HAPPY
- RELAXED
- RESTED
- SLEEPY
- APATHETIC
- SAD

Daily visualisation

In life: _____

In career: _____

In health/wellness: _____

The BIG goal I'm working towards today:

Today's priorities:

Top three mini goals:

1. _____

2. _____

3. _____

Reflection:

Today's three biggest wins:

1. _____

2. _____

3. _____

WEEKLY RECAP

"You can be soft and successful, a traditionalist and a rebel, a lover and a fighter, vulnerable and invincible."

@lisamessenger

Did I complete the past seven days?   Yes ☐   No ☐

If no, why did I miss the day/days: _____

_____

I can do better next week by: _____

_____

My best and/or biggest achievement of the week was:

_____

How is my progress is going towards your big goal?

_____

Reflection:

Some visualisation tools I used this week:

1. _____

2. _____

3. _____

My big actions for next week:

Rate your week: / 10

DAILY ACCOUNTABILITY

Today's mantra: I am mindful of my thoughts.

Date: ___ / ___ / _____

Today, I am feeling:

- EXCITED
- STRESSED
- ENERGETIC
- HAPPY
- RELAXED
- RESTED
- SLEEPY
- APATHETIC
- SAD

Daily visualisation

In life: _____

In career: _____

In health/wellness: _____

The BIG goal I'm working towards today:

Today's priorities:

Top three mini goals:

1. _____

2. _____

3. _____

Reflection:

Today's three biggest wins:

1. _____

2. _____

3. _____

DAILY ACCOUNTABILITY

Today's mantra: I will stop striving for perfection — good is good enough.

Date: ___ / ___ / _____

Today, I am feeling:

- EXCITED
- STRESSED
- ENERGETIC
- HAPPY
- RELAXED
- RESTED
- SLEEPY
- APATHETIC
- SAD

Daily visualisation

In life: _____

In career: _____

In health/wellness: _____

> The BIG goal I'm working towards today:

Today's priorities:

Top three mini goals:

1. _____

2. _____

3. _____

Reflection:

Today's three biggest wins:

1. _____

2. _____

3. _____

DAILY ACCOUNTABILITY

Today's mantra: I celebrate the growth that is coming my way.

Date: ___ / ___ / _____

Today, I am feeling:

- EXCITED
- STRESSED
- ENERGETIC
- HAPPY
- RELAXED
- RESTED
- SLEEPY
- APATHETIC
- SAD

Daily visualisation

In life: _____

In career: _____

In health/wellness: _____

The BIG goal I'm working towards today:

Today's priorities:

Top three mini goals:

1. _____

2. _____

3. _____

Reflection:

Today's three biggest wins:

1. _____

2. _____

3. _____

DAILY ACCOUNTABILITY

Today's mantra: I am ready to shine.

Date: ___ / ___ / _____

Today, I am feeling:

- EXCITED
- HAPPY
- SLEEPY
- STRESSED
- RELAXED
- APATHETIC
- ENERGETIC
- RESTED
- SAD

Daily visualisation

In life: _____

In career: _____

In health/wellness: _____

The BIG goal I'm working towards today:

Today's priorities:

Top three mini goals:

1. _____

2. _____

3. _____

Reflection:

Today's three biggest wins:

1. _____

2. _____

3. _____

DAILY ACCOUNTABILITY

Today's mantra: I will open my heart to change.

Date: ___ /___ /_____

Today, I am feeling:

- EXCITED
- STRESSED
- ENERGETIC

- HAPPY
- RELAXED
- RESTED

- SLEEPY
- APATHETIC
- SAD

Daily visualisation

In life: _____

In career: _____

In health/wellness: _____

The BIG goal I'm working towards today:

Today's priorities:

Top three mini goals:

1. _____

2. _____

3. _____

Reflection:

Today's three biggest wins:

1. _____

2. _____

3. _____

DAILY ACCOUNTABILITY

Today's mantra: This is exactly what I need.

Date: ___ /___ /_____

Today, I am feeling:

- EXCITED
- STRESSED
- ENERGETIC
- HAPPY
- RELAXED
- RESTED
- SLEEPY
- APATHETIC
- SAD

Daily visualisation

In life: _____

In career: _____

In health/wellness: _____

The BIG goal I'm working towards today:

Today's priorities:

Top three mini goals:

1. _____

2. _____

3. _____

Reflection:

Today's three biggest wins:

1. _____

2. _____

3. _____

DAILY ACCOUNTABILITY

Today's mantra: I am open to new possibilities.

Date: ___ / ___ / ____

Today, I am feeling:

- EXCITED
- STRESSED
- ENERGETIC
- HAPPY
- RELAXED
- RESTED
- SLEEPY
- APATHETIC
- SAD

Daily visualisation

In life: _____

In career: _____

In health/wellness: _____

The BIG goal I'm working towards today:

Today's priorities:

Top three mini goals:

1. _____

2. _____

3. _____

Reflection:

Today's three biggest wins:

1. _____

2. _____

3. _____

VISIONS & ACTIONS

WEEKLY RECAP

"Take that first step. Just imagine what you could be saying hello to. Hello future. Hello present. Hello friends. Hello career. Hello lover."

– Anon

Did I complete the past seven days?   Yes ☐   No ☐

If no, why did I miss the day/days: _____

_____

I can do better next week by: _____

_____

My best and/or biggest achievement of the week was:

_____

How is my progress is going towards your big goal?

_____

Reflection:

Some visualisation tools I used this week:

1. _____

2. _____

3. _____

My big actions for next week:

Rate your week: ___ / 10

DAILY ACCOUNTABILITY

Today's mantra: I am doing everything with purpose.

Date: ___ / ___ / _____

Today, I am feeling:

- EXCITED
- STRESSED
- ENERGETIC
- HAPPY
- RELAXED
- RESTED
- SLEEPY
- APATHETIC
- SAD

Daily visualisation

In life: _____

In career: _____

In health/wellness: _____

> The BIG goal I'm working towards today:

Today's priorities:

Top three mini goals:

1. _____

2. _____

3. _____

Reflection:

Today's three biggest wins:

1. _____

2. _____

3. _____

DAILY ACCOUNTABILITY

Today's mantra: I am grateful for all that I have.

Date: ___ / ___ / _____

Today, I am feeling:

- EXCITED
- STRESSED
- ENERGETIC
- HAPPY
- RELAXED
- RESTED
- SLEEPY
- APATHETIC
- SAD

Daily visualisation

In life: _____

In career: _____

In health/wellness: _____

The BIG goal I'm working towards today:

Today's priorities:

Top three mini goals:

1. _____

2. _____

3. _____

Reflection:

Today's three biggest wins:

1. _____

2. _____

3. _____

DAILY ACCOUNTABILITY

Today's mantra: My thoughts will become things.

Date: ___ / ___ / _____

Today, I am feeling:

- EXCITED
- STRESSED
- ENERGETIC
- HAPPY
- RELAXED
- RESTED
- SLEEPY
- APATHETIC
- SAD

Daily visualisation

In life: _____

In career: _____

In health/wellness: _____

The BIG goal I'm working towards today:

Today's priorities:

Top three mini goals:

1. _____

2. _____

3. _____

Reflection:

Today's three biggest wins:

1. _____

2. _____

3. _____

DAILY ACCOUNTABILITY

Today's mantra: I will live a life that I don't need to escape from.

Date: ___ /___ /_____

Today, I am feeling:

- EXCITED
- HAPPY
- SLEEPY
- STRESSED
- RELAXED
- APATHETIC
- ENERGETIC
- RESTED
- SAD

Daily visualisation

In life: _____

In career: _____

In health/wellness: _____

The BIG goal I'm working towards today:

Today's priorities:

Top three mini goals:

1. _____

2. _____

3. _____

Reflection:

Today's three biggest wins:

1. _____

2. _____

3. _____

DAILY ACCOUNTABILITY

Today's mantra: I am overflowing with joy, love and happiness.

Date: ___ / ___ / _____

Today, I am feeling:

- EXCITED
- STRESSED
- ENERGETIC

- HAPPY
- RELAXED
- RESTED

- SLEEPY
- APATHETIC
- SAD

Daily visualisation

In life: _____

In career: _____

In health/wellness: _____

The BIG goal I'm working towards today:

Today's priorities:

Top three mini goals:

1. _____

2. _____

3. _____

Reflection:

Today's three biggest wins:

1. _____

2. _____

3. _____

DAILY ACCOUNTABILITY

Today's mantra: I will choose strength in any situation.

Date: ___ /___ /____

Today, I am feeling:

- EXCITED
- STRESSED
- ENERGETIC
- HAPPY
- RELAXED
- RESTED
- SLEEPY
- APATHETIC
- SAD

Daily visualisation

In life: _____

In career: _____

In health/wellness: _____

The BIG goal I'm working towards today:

Today's priorities:

Top three mini goals:

1. _____

2. _____

3. _____

Reflection:

Today's three biggest wins:

1. _____

2. _____

3. _____

DAILY ACCOUNTABILITY

Today's mantra: There is no time to play small.

Date: ___ /___ /_____

Today, I am feeling:

- EXCITED
- STRESSED
- ENERGETIC
- HAPPY
- RELAXED
- RESTED
- SLEEPY
- APATHETIC
- SAD

Daily visualisation

In life: _____

In career: _____

In health/wellness: _____

The BIG goal I'm working towards today:

Today's priorities:

Top three mini goals:

1. _____

2. _____

3. _____

Reflection:

Today's three biggest wins:

1. _____

2. _____

3. _____

WEEKLY RECAP

*"Strength doesn't come from what you can do. It comes
from overcoming the things you once thought you couldn't."*

– Rikki Rogers

Did I complete the past seven days?   Yes ☐   No ☐

If no, why did I miss the day/days: _____

_____

I can do better next week by: _____

_____

My best and/or biggest achievement of the week was:

_____

How is my progress is going towards your big goal?

_____

Reflection:

Some visualisation tools I used this week:

1. _____

2. _____

3. _____

Rate your week: / 10

My big actions for next week:

DAILY ACCOUNTABILITY

Today's mantra: I embrace purpose and intent with open arms.

Date: ___ /___ /_____

Today, I am feeling:

- EXCITED
- HAPPY
- SLEEPY
- STRESSED
- RELAXED
- APATHETIC
- ENERGETIC
- RESTED
- SAD

Daily visualisation

In life: _____

In career: _____

In health/wellness: _____

The BIG goal I'm working towards today:

Today's priorities:

Top three mini goals:

1. _____

2. _____

3. _____

Reflection:

Today's three biggest wins:

1. _____

2. _____

3. _____

VISIONS & ACTIONS

DAILY ACCOUNTABILITY

Today's mantra: I am thankful for my abundance.

Date: ___ /___ /_____

Today, I am feeling:

- EXCITED
- STRESSED
- ENERGETIC
- HAPPY
- RELAXED
- RESTED
- SLEEPY
- APATHETIC
- SAD

Daily visualisation

In life: _____

In career: _____

In health/wellness: _____

```
The BIG goal I'm working towards today:



```

Today's priorities:

Top three mini goals:

1. _____

2. _____

3. _____

Reflection:

Today's three biggest wins:

1. _____

2. _____

3. _____

DAILY ACCOUNTABILITY

Today's mantra: I won't let fear stand in the way of success.

Date: ___ / ___ / _____

Today, I am feeling:

- EXCITED
- STRESSED
- ENERGETIC
- HAPPY
- RELAXED
- RESTED
- SLEEPY
- APATHETIC
- SAD

Daily visualisation

In life: _____

In career: _____

In health/wellness: _____

The BIG goal I'm working towards today:

Today's priorities:

Top three mini goals:

1. _____

2. _____

3. _____

Reflection:

Today's three biggest wins:

1. _____

2. _____

3. _____

DAILY ACCOUNTABILITY

Today's mantra: I am worthy of love, success and happiness.

Date: ___ /___ /_____

Today, I am feeling:

- EXCITED
- STRESSED
- ENERGETIC
- HAPPY
- RELAXED
- RESTED
- SLEEPY
- APATHETIC
- SAD

Daily visualisation

In life: _____

In career: _____

In health/wellness: _____

The BIG goal I'm working towards today:

Today's priorities:

Top three mini goals:

1. _____

2. _____

3. _____

Reflection:

Today's three biggest wins:

1. _____

2. _____

3. _____

DAILY ACCOUNTABILITY

Today's mantra: I am ready to accept anything that comes my way.

Date: ___ / ___ / _____

Today, I am feeling:

- EXCITED
- STRESSED
- ENERGETIC
- HAPPY
- RELAXED
- RESTED
- SLEEPY
- APATHETIC
- SAD

Daily visualisation

In life: _____

In career: _____

In health/wellness: _____

The BIG goal I'm working towards today:

Today's priorities:

Top three mini goals:

1. _____

2. _____

3. _____

Reflection:

Today's three biggest wins:

1. _____

2. _____

3. _____

DAILY ACCOUNTABILITY

Today's mantra: I am responsible for my actions.

Date: ___ /___ /_____

Today, I am feeling:

- EXCITED
- STRESSED
- ENERGETIC
- HAPPY
- RELAXED
- RESTED
- SLEEPY
- APATHETIC
- SAD

Daily visualisation

In life: _____

In career: _____

In health/wellness: _____

The BIG goal I'm working towards today:

Today's priorities:

Top three mini goals:

1. _____

2. _____

3. _____

Reflection:

Today's three biggest wins:

1. _____

2. _____

3. _____

DAILY ACCOUNTABILITY

Today's mantra: I will think before i act.

Date: ___ /___ /____

Today, I am feeling:

- EXCITED
- STRESSED
- ENERGETIC
- HAPPY
- RELAXED
- RESTED
- SLEEPY
- APATHETIC
- SAD

Daily visualisation

In life: _____

In career: _____

In health/wellness: _____

The BIG goal I'm working towards today:

Today's priorities:

Top three mini goals:

1. _____

2. _____

3. _____

Reflection:

Today's three biggest wins:

1. _____

2. _____

3. _____

WEEKLY RECAP

"If it's both terrifying and amazing, then you should pursue it."

– Erada

Did I complete the past seven days?   Yes ☐   No ☐

If no, why did I miss the day/days: _____

_____

I can do better next week by: _____

_____

My best and/or biggest achievement of the week was:

_____

How is my progress is going towards your big goal?

_____

Reflection:

Some visualisation tools I used this week:

1. _____

2. _____

3. _____

My big actions for next week:

Rate your week: ___ / 10

monthly review

"Almost everything will work again if you unplug it for a few minutes. Including you."

– Anne Lamott

The single biggest/best achievement for the month was:

I'm most proud of:

My best visualisation strategy was:

Three things I loved about this month:

1. _____

2. _____

3. _____

My healthiest action was:

My best career move/decision was:

My best mindset practice was:

I felt most successful/enlightened when:

The best moment of courage I had:

A visualisation that came true was:

Three things that didn't go to plan this month:

1. _____

2. _____

3. _____

How I can avoid or improve these things next month:

1. _____

2. _____

3. _____

Three visions and actions I undertook and achieved this month:

1. _____

2. _____

3. _____

"

Just let go.

Let go of how you thought your life should be, and embrace

the life that is trying to work its way into your consciousness.

"

Carolyn Myss

DAILY ACCOUNTABILITY

Today's mantra: I am choosing to look after me.

Date: ___ /___ /____

Today, I am feeling:

- EXCITED
- STRESSED
- ENERGETIC
- HAPPY
- RELAXED
- RESTED
- SLEEPY
- APATHETIC
- SAD

Daily visualisation

In life: _____

In career: _____

In health/wellness: _____

The BIG goal I'm working towards today:

Today's priorities:

Top three mini goals:

1. _____

2. _____

3. _____

Reflection:

Today's three biggest wins:

1. _____

2. _____

3. _____

DAILY ACCOUNTABILITY

Today's mantra: I am ready to make today count.

Date: ___ / ___ / _____

Today, I am feeling:

- EXCITED
- STRESSED
- ENERGETIC
- HAPPY
- RELAXED
- RESTED
- SLEEPY
- APATHETIC
- SAD

Daily visualisation

In life: _____

In career: _____

In health/wellness: _____

The BIG goal I'm working towards today:

Today's priorities:

Top three mini goals:

1. _____

2. _____

3. _____

Reflection:

Today's three biggest wins:

1. _____

2. _____

3. _____

DAILY ACCOUNTABILITY

Today's mantra: I will embrace the beauty all around me.

Date: ___ /___ /____

Today, I am feeling:

- EXCITED
- STRESSED
- ENERGETIC
- HAPPY
- RELAXED
- RESTED
- SLEEPY
- APATHETIC
- SAD

Daily visualisation

In life: _____

In career: _____

In health/wellness: _____

The BIG goal I'm working towards today:

Today's priorities:

Top three mini goals:

1. _____

2. _____

3. _____

Reflection:

Today's three biggest wins:

1. _____

2. _____

3. _____

DAILY ACCOUNTABILITY

Today's mantra: I will express my gratitude openly.

Date: ___ / ___ / _____

Today, I am feeling:

- EXCITED
- STRESSED
- ENERGETIC
- HAPPY
- RELAXED
- RESTED
- SLEEPY
- APATHETIC
- SAD

Daily visualisation

In life: _____

In career: _____

In health/wellness: _____

> The BIG goal I'm working towards today:

Today's priorities:

Top three mini goals:

1. _____

2. _____

3. _____

Reflection:

Today's three biggest wins:

1. _____

2. _____

3. _____

DAILY ACCOUNTABILITY

Today's mantra: I have faith in what is to come.

Date: ___ / ___ / _____

Today, I am feeling:

- EXCITED
- STRESSED
- ENERGETIC
- HAPPY
- RELAXED
- RESTED
- SLEEPY
- APATHETIC
- SAD

Daily visualisation

In life: _____

In career: _____

In health/wellness: _____

The BIG goal I'm working towards today:

Today's priorities:

Top three mini goals:

1. _____

2. _____

3. _____

Reflection:

Today's three biggest wins:

1. _____

2. _____

3. _____

DAILY ACCOUNTABILITY

Today's mantra: I am ready to step into authenticity.

Date: ___ /___ /_____

Today, I am feeling:

- EXCITED
- STRESSED
- ENERGETIC
- HAPPY
- RELAXED
- RESTED
- SLEEPY
- APATHETIC
- SAD

Daily visualisation

In life: _____

In career: _____

In health/wellness: _____

The BIG goal I'm working towards today:

Today's priorities:

Top three mini goals:

1. _____

2. _____

3. _____

Reflection:

Today's three biggest wins:

1. _____

2. _____

3. _____

DAILY ACCOUNTABILITY

Today's mantra: I will stop and listen.

Date: ___ /___ /_____

Today, I am feeling:

- EXCITED
- STRESSED
- ENERGETIC
- HAPPY
- RELAXED
- RESTED
- SLEEPY
- APATHETIC
- SAD

Daily visualisation

In life: _____

In career: _____

In health/wellness: _____

The BIG goal I'm working towards today:

Today's priorities:

Top three mini goals:

1. _____

2. _____

3. _____

Reflection:

Today's three biggest wins:

1. _____

2. _____

3. _____

WEEKLY RECAP

"Imagine if you stopped focusing on your problems and started focusing on the possibilities."

– Anon

Did I complete the past seven days?   Yes ☐   No ☐

If no, why did I miss the day/days: _____

_____

I can do better next week by: _____

_____

My best and/or biggest achievement of the week was:

_____

How is my progress is going towards your big goal?

_____

Reflection:

Some visualisation tools I used this week:

1. _____

2. _____

3. _____

Rate your week: ⌀ /10

My big actions for next week:

DAILY ACCOUNTABILITY

Today's mantra: Today will be filled with positivity.

Date: ___ / ___ / _____

Today, I am feeling:

- EXCITED
- STRESSED
- ENERGETIC
- HAPPY
- RELAXED
- RESTED
- SLEEPY
- APATHETIC
- SAD

Daily visualisation

In life: _____

In career: _____

In health/wellness: _____

The BIG goal I'm working towards today:

Today's priorities:

Top three mini goals:

1. _____

2. _____

3. _____

Reflection:

Today's three biggest wins:

1. _____

2. _____

3. _____

DAILY ACCOUNTABILITY

Today's mantra: I possess the power to make today truly great.

Date: ___ /___ /_____

Today, I am feeling:

- EXCITED
- STRESSED
- ENERGETIC
- HAPPY
- RELAXED
- RESTED
- SLEEPY
- APATHETIC
- SAD

Daily visualisation

In life: _____

In career: _____

In health/wellness: _____

The BIG goal I'm working towards today:

Today's priorities:

Top three mini goals:

1. _____

2. _____

3. _____

Reflection:

Today's three biggest wins:

1. _____

2. _____

3. _____

DAILY ACCOUNTABILITY

Today's mantra: I am at peace with uncertainty.

Date: ___ /___ /_____

Today, I am feeling:

- EXCITED
- STRESSED
- ENERGETIC
- HAPPY
- RELAXED
- RESTED
- SLEEPY
- APATHETIC
- SAD

Daily visualisation

In life: _____

In career: _____

In health/wellness: _____

The BIG goal I'm working towards today:

Today's priorities:

Top three mini goals:

1. _____

2. _____

3. _____

Reflection:

Today's three biggest wins:

1. _____

2. _____

3. _____

DAILY ACCOUNTABILITY

Today's mantra: I will intentionally make time for me.

Date: ___ / ___ / _____

Today, I am feeling:

- EXCITED
- STRESSED
- ENERGETIC
- HAPPY
- RELAXED
- RESTED
- SLEEPY
- APATHETIC
- SAD

Daily visualisation

In life: _____

In career: _____

In health/wellness: _____

The BIG goal I'm working towards today:

Today's priorities:

Top three mini goals:

1. _____

2. _____

3. _____

Reflection:

Today's three biggest wins:

1. _____

2. _____

3. _____

DAILY ACCOUNTABILITY

Today's mantra: My mistakes are my lessons.

Date: ___ /___ /_____

Today, I am feeling:

- EXCITED
- STRESSED
- ENERGETIC
- HAPPY
- RELAXED
- RESTED
- SLEEPY
- APATHETIC
- SAD

Daily visualisation

In life: _____

In career: _____

In health/wellness: _____

The BIG goal I'm working towards today:

Today's priorities:

Top three mini goals:

1. _____

2. _____

3. _____

Reflection:

Today's three biggest wins:

1. _____

2. _____

3. _____

DAILY ACCOUNTABILITY

Today's mantra: I choose to show up wholeheartedly.

Date: ___ /___ /_____

Today, I am feeling:

- EXCITED
- STRESSED
- ENERGETIC
- HAPPY
- RELAXED
- RESTED
- SLEEPY
- APATHETIC
- SAD

Daily visualisation

In life: _____

In career: _____

In health/wellness: _____

The BIG goal I'm working towards today:

Today's priorities:

Top three mini goals:

1. _____

2. _____

3. _____

Reflection:

Today's three biggest wins:

1. _____

2. _____

3. _____

DAILY ACCOUNTABILITY

Today's mantra: I am unique.

Date: ___ / ___ / _____

Today, I am feeling:

- EXCITED
- HAPPY
- SLEEPY
- STRESSED
- RELAXED
- APATHETIC
- ENERGETIC
- RESTED
- SAD

Daily visualisation

In life: _____

In career: _____

In health/wellness: _____

The BIG goal I'm working towards today:

Today's priorities:

Top three mini goals:

1. _____

2. _____

3. _____

Reflection:

Today's three biggest wins:

1. _____

2. _____

3. _____

WEEKLY RECAP

"You are a series of mistakes that had to happen for you to find you."

– Atticus

Did I complete the past seven days?   Yes ☐   No ☐

If no, why did I miss the day/days: _____

_____

I can do better next week by: _____

_____

My best and/or biggest achievement of the week was:

_____

How is my progress is going towards your big goal?

_____

Reflection:

Some visualisation tools I used this week:

1. _____

2. _____

3. _____

My big actions for next week:

Rate your week: / 10

DAILY ACCOUNTABILITY

Today's mantra: I can do anything I put my mind to.

Date: ___ / ___ / _____

Today, I am feeling:

- EXCITED
- STRESSED
- ENERGETIC
- HAPPY
- RELAXED
- RESTED
- SLEEPY
- APATHETIC
- SAD

Daily visualisation

In life: _____

In career: _____

In health/wellness: _____

The BIG goal I'm working towards today:

Today's priorities:

Top three mini goals:

1. _____

2. _____

3. _____

Reflection:

Today's three biggest wins:

1. _____

2. _____

3. _____

DAILY ACCOUNTABILITY

Today's mantra: I am ready to embrace my strength.

Date: ___ /___ /_____

Today, I am feeling:

- EXCITED
- HAPPY
- SLEEPY
- STRESSED
- RELAXED
- APATHETIC
- ENERGETIC
- RESTED
- SAD

Daily visualisation

In life: _____

In career: _____

In health/wellness: _____

> The BIG goal I'm working towards today:

Today's priorities:

Top three mini goals:

1. _____

2. _____

3. _____

Reflection:

Today's three biggest wins:

1. _____

2. _____

3. _____

DAILY ACCOUNTABILITY

Today's mantra: I will be kind to everyone, no matter what happens.

Date: ___ /___ /_____

Today, I am feeling:

- EXCITED
- STRESSED
- ENERGETIC
- HAPPY
- RELAXED
- RESTED
- SLEEPY
- APATHETIC
- SAD

Daily visualisation

In life: _____

In career: _____

In health/wellness: _____

```
The BIG goal I'm working towards today:



```

Today's priorities:

Top three mini goals:

1. _____

2. _____

3. _____

Reflection:

Today's three biggest wins:

1. _____

2. _____

3. _____

VISIONS & ACTIONS

DAILY ACCOUNTABILITY

Today's mantra: It's okay to let go.

Date: ___ /___ /_____

Today, I am feeling:

- EXCITED
- STRESSED
- ENERGETIC
- HAPPY
- RELAXED
- RESTED
- SLEEPY
- APATHETIC
- SAD

Daily visualisation

In life: _____

In career: _____

In health/wellness: _____

The BIG goal I'm working towards today:

Today's priorities:

Top three mini goals:

1. _____

2. _____

3. _____

Reflection:

Today's three biggest wins:

1. _____

2. _____

3. _____

DAILY ACCOUNTABILITY

Today's mantra: I will be brave in unpredictable moments.

Date: ___ / ___ / _____

Today, I am feeling:

- EXCITED
- STRESSED
- ENERGETIC
- HAPPY
- RELAXED
- RESTED
- SLEEPY
- APATHETIC
- SAD

Daily visualisation

In life: _____

In career: _____

In health/wellness: _____

The BIG goal I'm working towards today:

Today's priorities:

Top three mini goals:

1. _____

2. _____

3. _____

Reflection:

Today's three biggest wins:

1. _____

2. _____

3. _____

DAILY ACCOUNTABILITY

Today's mantra: I release anyone who limits my potential.

Date: ___ / ___ / _____

Today, I am feeling:

- EXCITED
- STRESSED
- ENERGETIC
- HAPPY
- RELAXED
- RESTED
- SLEEPY
- APATHETIC
- SAD

Daily visualisation

In life: _____

In career: _____

In health/wellness: _____

The BIG goal I'm working towards today:

Today's priorities:

Top three mini goals:

1. _____

2. _____

3. _____

Reflection:

Today's three biggest wins:

1. _____

2. _____

3. _____

DAILY ACCOUNTABILITY

Today's mantra: I will do my best to support everyone around me.

Date: ___ / ___ / ____

Today, I am feeling:

- EXCITED
- STRESSED
- ENERGETIC
- HAPPY
- RELAXED
- RESTED
- SLEEPY
- APATHETIC
- SAD

Daily visualisation

In life: _____

In career: _____

In health/wellness: _____

The BIG goal I'm working towards today:

Today's priorities:

Top three mini goals:

1. _____

2. _____

3. _____

Reflection:

Today's three biggest wins:

1. _____

2. _____

3. _____

WEEKLY RECAP

"They told me I couldn't. So I did."

– Anon

Did I complete the past seven days? Yes ☐ No ☐

If no, why did I miss the day/days: _____

_____

I can do better next week by: _____

_____

My best and/or biggest achievement of the week was:

_____

How is my progress is going towards your big goal?

_____

Reflection:

Some visualisation tools I used this week:

1. _____

2. _____

3. _____

Rate your week: /10

My big actions for next week:

DAILY ACCOUNTABILITY

Today's mantra: I am ready to make my dreams a reality.

Date: ___ / ___ / _____

Today, I am feeling:

- EXCITED
- STRESSED
- ENERGETIC
- HAPPY
- RELAXED
- RESTED
- SLEEPY
- APATHETIC
- SAD

Daily visualisation

In life: _____

In career: _____

In health/wellness: _____

The BIG goal I'm working towards today:

Today's priorities:

Top three mini goals:

1. _____

2. _____

3. _____

Reflection:

Today's three biggest wins:

1. _____

2. _____

3. _____

DAILY ACCOUNTABILITY

Today's mantra: This is the first day of the rest of my life.

Date: ___ /___ /_____

Today, I am feeling:

- EXCITED
- STRESSED
- ENERGETIC

- HAPPY
- RELAXED
- RESTED

- SLEEPY
- APATHETIC
- SAD

Daily visualisation

In life: _____

In career: _____

In health/wellness: _____

The BIG goal I'm working towards today:

Today's priorities:

Top three mini goals:

1. _____

2. _____

3. _____

Reflection:

Today's three biggest wins:

1. _____

2. _____

3. _____

JOURNALING

DAILY ACCOUNTABILITY

Today's mantra: I will treasure each day as though it's my last.

Date: ___ / ___ / _____

Today, I am feeling:

- EXCITED
- HAPPY
- SLEEPY
- STRESSED
- RELAXED
- APATHETIC
- ENERGETIC
- RESTED
- SAD

Daily visualisation

In life: _____

In career: _____

In health/wellness: _____

The BIG goal I'm working towards today:

Today's priorities:

Top three mini goals:

1. _____

2. _____

3. _____

Reflection:

Today's three biggest wins:

1. _____

2. _____

3. _____

DAILY ACCOUNTABILITY

Today's mantra: I will make the future me the best version possible.

Date: ___ /___ /_____

Today, I am feeling:

- EXCITED
- HAPPY
- SLEEPY
- STRESSED
- RELAXED
- APATHETIC
- ENERGETIC
- RESTED
- SAD

Daily visualisation

In life: _____

In career: _____

In health/wellness: _____

The BIG goal I'm working towards today:

Today's priorities:

Top three mini goals:

1. _____

2. _____

3. _____

Reflection:

Today's three biggest wins:

1. _____

2. _____

3. _____

DAILY ACCOUNTABILITY

Today's mantra: I am unashamedly me.

Date: ___ / ___ / _____

Today, I am feeling:

- EXCITED
- STRESSED
- ENERGETIC
- HAPPY
- RELAXED
- RESTED
- SLEEPY
- APATHETIC
- SAD

Daily visualisation

In life: _____

In career: _____

In health/wellness: _____

The BIG goal I'm working towards today:

Today's priorities:

Top three mini goals:

1. _____

2. _____

3. _____

Reflection:

Today's three biggest wins:

1. _____

2. _____

3. _____

DAILY ACCOUNTABILITY

Today's mantra: I love my body and all it does for me.

Date: ___ /___ /_____

Today, I am feeling:

- EXCITED
- STRESSED
- ENERGETIC
- HAPPY
- RELAXED
- RESTED
- SLEEPY
- APATHETIC
- SAD

Daily visualisation

In life: _____

In career: _____

In health/wellness: _____

The BIG goal I'm working towards today:

Today's priorities:

Top three mini goals:

1. _____

2. _____

3. _____

Reflection:

Today's three biggest wins:

1. _____

2. _____

3. _____

DAILY ACCOUNTABILITY

Today's mantra: I will embrace the ebbs and flows of life.

Date: ___ / ___ / ____

Today, I am feeling:

- EXCITED
- STRESSED
- ENERGETIC
- HAPPY
- RELAXED
- RESTED
- SLEEPY
- APATHETIC
- SAD

Daily visualisation

In life: _____

In career: _____

In health/wellness: _____

The BIG goal I'm working towards today:

Today's priorities:

Top three mini goals:

1. _____

2. _____

3. _____

Reflection:

Today's three biggest wins:

1. _____

2. _____

3. _____

WEEKLY RECAP

"Fall in love with your future, because it's yours to create."

@collectivehub

Did I complete the past seven days?   Yes ☐   No ☐

If no, why did I miss the day/days: _____

_____

I can do better next week by: _____

_____

My best and/or biggest achievement of the week was:

_____

How is my progress is going towards your big goal?

_____

Reflection:

Some visualisation tools I used this week:

1. _____

2. _____

3. _____

Rate your week: / 10

My big actions for next week:

monthly review

"Eventually all things fall into place. Until then, laugh at the confusion, live for the moments, and know that everything happens for a reason."

– Albert Schweitzer

The single biggest/best achievement for the month was:
_____
_____
_____
_____

I'm most proud of:
_____
_____
_____
_____

My best visualisation strategy was:
_____
_____
_____
_____
_____

Three things I loved about this month:

1. _____

2. _____

3. _____

My healthiest action was:

My best career move/decision was:

My best mindset practice was:

I felt most successful/enlightened when:

The best moment of courage I had:

A visualisation that came true was:

Three things that didn't go to plan this month:

1. _____

2. _____

3. _____

How I can avoid or improve these things next month:

1. _____

2. _____

3. _____

Three visions and actions I undertook and achieved this month:

1. _____

2. _____

3. _____

> **Read more books than status updates.
> Look into more eyes than screens.**

Hold more hands than devices. Love more than you judge.

,,

– Anon

DAILY ACCOUNTABILITY

Today's mantra: I will not judge others.

Date: ___ /___ /_____

Today, I am feeling:

- EXCITED
- STRESSED
- ENERGETIC
- HAPPY
- RELAXED
- RESTED
- SLEEPY
- APATHETIC
- SAD

Daily visualisation

In life: _____

In career: _____

In health/wellness: _____

The BIG goal I'm working towards today:

Today's priorities:

Top three mini goals:

1. _____

2. _____

3. _____

Reflection:

Today's three biggest wins:

1. _____

2. _____

3. _____

DAILY ACCOUNTABILITY

Today's mantra: New and exciting adventures are coming.

Date: ___ /___ /_____

Today, I am feeling:

- EXCITED
- STRESSED
- ENERGETIC
- HAPPY
- RELAXED
- RESTED
- SLEEPY
- APATHETIC
- SAD

Daily visualisation

In life: _____

In career: _____

In health/wellness: _____

> The BIG goal I'm working towards today:

Today's priorities:

Top three mini goals:

1. _____

2. _____

3. _____

Reflection:

Today's three biggest wins:

1. _____

2. _____

3. _____

DAILY ACCOUNTABILITY

Today's mantra: I am scheduling 'me time'.

Date: ___ /___ /_____

Today, I am feeling:

- EXCITED
- STRESSED
- ENERGETIC
- HAPPY
- RELAXED
- RESTED
- SLEEPY
- APATHETIC
- SAD

Daily visualisation

In life: _____

In career: _____

In health/wellness: _____

```
The BIG goal I'm working towards today:



```

Today's priorities:

Top three mini goals:

1. _____

2. _____

3. _____

Reflection:

Today's three biggest wins:

1. _____

2. _____

3. _____

DAILY ACCOUNTABILITY

Today's mantra: I have loved once and I will love again.

Date: ___ /___ /_____

Today, I am feeling:

- EXCITED
- STRESSED
- ENERGETIC
- HAPPY
- RELAXED
- RESTED
- SLEEPY
- APATHETIC
- SAD

Daily visualisation

In life: _____

In career: _____

In health/wellness: _____

The BIG goal I'm working towards today:

Today's priorities:

Top three mini goals:

1. _____

2. _____

3. _____

Reflection:

Today's three biggest wins:

1. _____

2. _____

3. _____

DAILY ACCOUNTABILITY

Today's mantra: I will achieve all my goals for today.

Date: ___ /___ /_____

Today, I am feeling:

- EXCITED
- STRESSED
- ENERGETIC
- HAPPY
- RELAXED
- RESTED
- SLEEPY
- APATHETIC
- SAD

Daily visualisation

In life: _____

In career: _____

In health/wellness: _____

The BIG goal I'm working towards today:

Today's priorities:

Top three mini goals:

1. _____

2. _____

3. _____

Reflection:

Today's three biggest wins:

1. _____

2. _____

3. _____

DAILY ACCOUNTABILITY

Today's mantra: I have no doubts in my decisions.

Date: ___ /___ /____

Today, I am feeling:

- EXCITED
- STRESSED
- ENERGETIC
- HAPPY
- RELAXED
- RESTED
- SLEEPY
- APATHETIC
- SAD

Daily visualisation

In life: _____

In career: _____

In health/wellness: _____

```
The BIG goal I'm working towards today:
```

Today's priorities:

Top three mini goals:

1. _____

2. _____

3. _____

Reflection:

Today's three biggest wins:

1. _____

2. _____

3. _____

DAILY ACCOUNTABILITY

Today's mantra: I will live beyond the boundaries of ordinary.

Date: ___ / ___ / ____

Today, I am feeling:

- EXCITED
- STRESSED
- ENERGETIC
- HAPPY
- RELAXED
- RESTED
- SLEEPY
- APATHETIC
- SAD

Daily visualisation

In life: _____

In career: _____

In health/wellness: _____

The BIG goal I'm working towards today:

Today's priorities:

Top three mini goals:

1. _____

2. _____

3. _____

Reflection:

Today's three biggest wins:

1. _____

2. _____

3. _____

WEEKLY RECAP

"She was unstoppable. Not because she didn't have failures or doubts. But because she continued on despite them."

– Anon

Did I complete the past seven days? Yes ☐ No ☐

If no, why did I miss the day/days: _____

_____

I can do better next week by: _____

_____

My best and/or biggest achievement of the week was:

_____

How is my progress is going towards your big goal?

_____

Reflection:

Some visualisation tools I used this week:

1. _____

2. _____

3. _____

My big actions for next week:

Rate your week: /10

DAILY ACCOUNTABILITY

Today's mantra: I will expand my knowledge and understanding.

Date: ___ /___ /_____

Today, I am feeling:

- EXCITED
- STRESSED
- ENERGETIC
- HAPPY
- RELAXED
- RESTED
- SLEEPY
- APATHETIC
- SAD

Daily visualisation

In life: _____

In career: _____

In health/wellness: _____

> The BIG goal I'm working towards today:

Today's priorities:

Top three mini goals:

1. _____

2. _____

3. _____

Reflection:

Today's three biggest wins:

1. _____

2. _____

3. _____

DAILY ACCOUNTABILITY

Today's mantra: Good things are coming.

Date: ___ /___ /_____

Today, I am feeling:

- EXCITED
- STRESSED
- ENERGETIC
- HAPPY
- RELAXED
- RESTED
- SLEEPY
- APATHETIC
- SAD

Daily visualisation

In life: _____

In career: _____

In health/wellness: _____

The BIG goal I'm working towards today:

Today's priorities:

Top three mini goals:

1. _____

2. _____

3. _____

Reflection:

Today's three biggest wins:

1. _____

2. _____

3. _____

DAILY ACCOUNTABILITY

Today's mantra: Life is full of beauty and uncertainty.

Date: ___ / ___ / ____

Today, I am feeling:

- EXCITED
- STRESSED
- ENERGETIC
- HAPPY
- RELAXED
- RESTED
- SLEEPY
- APATHETIC
- SAD

Daily visualisation

In life: _____

In career: _____

In health/wellness: _____

> The BIG goal I'm working towards today:

Today's priorities:

Top three mini goals:

1. _____

2. _____

3. _____

Reflection:

Today's three biggest wins:

1. _____

2. _____

3. _____

DAILY ACCOUNTABILITY

Today's mantra: I value my health.

Date: ___ /___ /____

Today, I am feeling:

- EXCITED
- STRESSED
- ENERGETIC
- HAPPY
- RELAXED
- RESTED
- SLEEPY
- APATHETIC
- SAD

Daily visualisation

In life: _____

In career: _____

In health/wellness: _____

The BIG goal I'm working towards today:

Today's priorities:

Top three mini goals:

1. _____

2. _____

3. _____

Reflection:

Today's three biggest wins:

1. _____

2. _____

3. _____

DAILY ACCOUNTABILITY

Today's mantra: I will fill my body with nutritional foods.

Date: ___ /___ /_____

Today, I am feeling:

- EXCITED
- STRESSED
- ENERGETIC
- HAPPY
- RELAXED
- RESTED
- SLEEPY
- APATHETIC
- SAD

Daily visualisation

In life: _____

In career: _____

In health/wellness: _____

The BIG goal I'm working towards today:

Today's priorities:

Top three mini goals:

1. _____

2. _____

3. _____

Reflection:

Today's three biggest wins:

1. _____

2. _____

3. _____

DAILY ACCOUNTABILITY

Today's mantra: I owe it to myself to take a break.

Date: ___ /___ /_____

Today, I am feeling:

- EXCITED
- STRESSED
- ENERGETIC
- HAPPY
- RELAXED
- RESTED
- SLEEPY
- APATHETIC
- SAD

Daily visualisation

In life: _____

In career: _____

In health/wellness: _____

The BIG goal I'm working towards today:

Today's priorities:

Top three mini goals:

1. _____

2. _____

3. _____

Reflection:

Today's three biggest wins:

1. _____

2. _____

3. _____

DAILY ACCOUNTABILITY

Today's mantra: I will survive.

Date: __ / __ / ____

Today, I am feeling:

- EXCITED
- STRESSED
- ENERGETIC
- HAPPY
- RELAXED
- RESTED
- SLEEPY
- APATHETIC
- SAD

Daily visualisation

In life: _____

In career: _____

In health/wellness: _____

The BIG goal I'm working towards today:

Today's priorities:

Top three mini goals:

1. _____

2. _____

3. _____

Reflection:

Today's three biggest wins:

1. _____

2. _____

3. _____

WEEKLY RECAP

"Solitude is important; it's necessary sometimes, if not often, to be away from society, surrounded by the things that bring you peace."

– Scottie Waves

Did I complete the past seven days?   Yes ☐   No ☐

If no, why did I miss the day/days: _____

_____

I can do better next week by: _____

_____

My best and/or biggest achievement of the week was:

_____

How is my progress is going towards your big goal?

_____

Reflection:

Some visualisation tools I used this week:

1. _____

2. _____

3. _____

My big actions for next week:

Rate your week: ___ / 10

DAILY ACCOUNTABILITY

Today's mantra: I will clear my mind and focus on the calm.

Date: ___ / ___ / _____

Today, I am feeling:

- EXCITED
- STRESSED
- ENERGETIC
- HAPPY
- RELAXED
- RESTED
- SLEEPY
- APATHETIC
- SAD

Daily visualisation

In life: _____

In career: _____

In health/wellness: _____

The BIG goal I'm working towards today:

Today's priorities:

Top three mini goals:

1. _____

2. _____

3. _____

Reflection:

Today's three biggest wins:

1. _____

2. _____

3. _____

DAILY ACCOUNTABILITY

Today's mantra: I am stronger every day.

Date: ___ / ___ / _____

Today, I am feeling:

- EXCITED
- STRESSED
- ENERGETIC
- HAPPY
- RELAXED
- RESTED
- SLEEPY
- APATHETIC
- SAD

Daily visualisation

In life: _____

In career: _____

In health/wellness: _____

The BIG goal I'm working towards today:

Today's priorities:

Top three mini goals:

1. _____

2. _____

3. _____

Reflection:

Today's three biggest wins:

1. _____

2. _____

3. _____

DAILY ACCOUNTABILITY

Today's mantra: I will empower myself with positive thoughts.

Date: ___ / ___ / _____

Today, I am feeling:

- EXCITED
- STRESSED
- ENERGETIC
- HAPPY
- RELAXED
- RESTED
- SLEEPY
- APATHETIC
- SAD

Daily visualisation

In life: _____

In career: _____

In health/wellness: _____

The BIG goal I'm working towards today:

Today's priorities:

Top three mini goals:

1. _____

2. _____

3. _____

Reflection:

Today's three biggest wins:

1. _____

2. _____

3. _____

DAILY ACCOUNTABILITY

Today's mantra: I will share my skills with people around me.

Date: ___ /___ /_____

Today, I am feeling:

- EXCITED
- HAPPY
- SLEEPY
- STRESSED
- RELAXED
- APATHETIC
- ENERGETIC
- RESTED
- SAD

Daily visualisation

In life: _____

In career: _____

In health/wellness: _____

> The BIG goal I'm working towards today:

Today's priorities:

Top three mini goals:

1. _____

2. _____

3. _____

Reflection:

Today's three biggest wins:

1. _____

2. _____

3. _____

DAILY ACCOUNTABILITY

Today's mantra: I will not let others' dramas affect me.

Date: ___ / ___ / _____

Today, I am feeling:

- EXCITED
- STRESSED
- ENERGETIC

- HAPPY
- RELAXED
- RESTED

- SLEEPY
- APATHETIC
- SAD

Daily visualisation

In life: _____

In career: _____

In health/wellness: _____

The BIG goal I'm working towards today:

Today's priorities:

Top three mini goals:

1. _____

2. _____

3. _____

Reflection:

Today's three biggest wins:

1. _____

2. _____

3. _____

DAILY ACCOUNTABILITY

Today's mantra: I am accountable for my actions.

Date: ___ / ___ / _____

Today, I am feeling:

- EXCITED
- STRESSED
- ENERGETIC
- HAPPY
- RELAXED
- RESTED
- SLEEPY
- APATHETIC
- SAD

Daily visualisation

In life: _____

In career: _____

In health/wellness: _____

The BIG goal I'm working towards today:

Today's priorities:

Top three mini goals:

1. _____

2. _____

3. _____

Reflection:

Today's three biggest wins:

1. _____

2. _____

3. _____

DAILY ACCOUNTABILITY

Today's mantra: I am taking control of my life.

Date: ___ / ___ / _____

Today, I am feeling:

- EXCITED
- STRESSED
- ENERGETIC

- HAPPY
- RELAXED
- RESTED

- SLEEPY
- APATHETIC
- SAD

Daily visualisation

In life: _____

In career: _____

In health/wellness: _____

The BIG goal I'm working towards today:

Today's priorities:

Top three mini goals:

1. _____

2. _____

3. _____

Reflection:

Today's three biggest wins:

1. _____

2. _____

3. _____

WEEKLY RECAP

"Make the decision. Do the thing. The universe will reward you for your bravery. Maybe today, maybe a week from now — but until you make the change the universe is keeping your next round on ice."

– Sarah Nally

Did I complete the past seven days?   Yes ☐   No ☐

If no, why did I miss the day/days: _____

_____

I can do better next week by: _____

_____

My best and/or biggest achievement of the week was:

_____

How is my progress is going towards your big goal?

_____

Reflection:

Some visualisation tools I used this week:

1. _____

2. _____

3. _____

My big actions for next week:

Rate your week: ___ / 10

DAILY ACCOUNTABILITY

Today's mantra: Yesterday is my only competition.

Date: ___ /___ /_____

Today, I am feeling:

- EXCITED
- HAPPY
- SLEEPY
- STRESSED
- RELAXED
- APATHETIC
- ENERGETIC
- RESTED
- SAD

Daily visualisation

In life: _____

In career: _____

In health/wellness: _____

> The BIG goal I'm working towards today:

Today's priorities:

Top three mini goals:

1. _____

2. _____

3. _____

Reflection:

Today's three biggest wins:

1. _____

2. _____

3. _____

DAILY ACCOUNTABILITY

Today's mantra: I am a darer and a doer.

Date: ___ /___ /_____

Today, I am feeling:

- EXCITED
- STRESSED
- ENERGETIC
- HAPPY
- RELAXED
- RESTED
- SLEEPY
- APATHETIC
- SAD

Daily visualisation

In life: _____

In career: _____

In health/wellness: _____

The BIG goal I'm working towards today:

Today's priorities:

Top three mini goals:

1. _____

2. _____

3. _____

Reflection:

Today's three biggest wins:

1. _____

2. _____

3. _____

DAILY ACCOUNTABILITY

Today's mantra: I will try my best to inspire others.

Date: ___ / ___ / _____

Today, I am feeling:

- EXCITED
- STRESSED
- ENERGETIC
- HAPPY
- RELAXED
- RESTED
- SLEEPY
- APATHETIC
- SAD

Daily visualisation

In life: _____

In career: _____

In health/wellness: _____

The BIG goal I'm working towards today:

Today's priorities:

Top three mini goals:

1. _____

2. _____

3. _____

Reflection:

Today's three biggest wins:

1. _____

2. _____

3. _____

DAILY ACCOUNTABILITY

Today's mantra: I will face my fears.

Date: ___ /___ /_____

Today, I am feeling:

- EXCITED
- STRESSED
- ENERGETIC
- HAPPY
- RELAXED
- RESTED
- SLEEPY
- APATHETIC
- SAD

Daily visualisation

In life: _____

In career: _____

In health/wellness: _____

> The BIG goal I'm working towards today:

Today's priorities:

Top three mini goals:

1. _____

2. _____

3. _____

Reflection:

Today's three biggest wins:

1. _____

2. _____

3. _____

DAILY ACCOUNTABILITY

Today's mantra: I will help and support a friend in need.

Date: ___ / ___ / ____

Today, I am feeling:

- EXCITED
- STRESSED
- ENERGETIC
- HAPPY
- RELAXED
- RESTED
- SLEEPY
- APATHETIC
- SAD

Daily visualisation

In life: _____

In career: _____

In health/wellness: _____

The BIG goal I'm working towards today:

Today's priorities:

Top three mini goals:

1. _____

2. _____

3. _____

Reflection:

Today's three biggest wins:

1. _____

2. _____

3. _____

DAILY ACCOUNTABILITY

Today's mantra: I will attract what I want in my life.

Date: ___ /___ /_____

Today, I am feeling:

- EXCITED
- STRESSED
- ENERGETIC
- HAPPY
- RELAXED
- RESTED
- SLEEPY
- APATHETIC
- SAD

Daily visualisation

In life: _____

In career: _____

In health/wellness: _____

The BIG goal I'm working towards today:

Today's priorities:

Top three mini goals:

1. _____

2. _____

3. _____

Reflection:

Today's three biggest wins:

1. _____

2. _____

3. _____

DAILY ACCOUNTABILITY

Today's mantra: I am selfless.

Date: ___ /___ /____

Today, I am feeling:

- EXCITED
- STRESSED
- ENERGETIC
- HAPPY
- RELAXED
- RESTED
- SLEEPY
- APATHETIC
- SAD

Daily visualisation

In life: _____

In career: _____

In health/wellness: _____

The BIG goal I'm working towards today:

Today's priorities:

Top three mini goals:

1. _____

2. _____

3. _____

Reflection:

Today's three biggest wins:

1. _____

2. _____

3. _____

WEEKLY RECAP

"If you really want something, and really work hard, and take advantage of opportunities, and never give up, you will find a way."

– Dr Jane Goodall

Did I complete the past seven days? Yes ☐   No ☐

If no, why did I miss the day/days: _____

_____

I can do better next week by: _____

_____

My best and/or biggest achievement of the week was:

_____

How is my progress is going towards your big goal?

_____

Reflection:

Some visualisation tools I used this week:

1. _____

2. _____

3. _____

My big actions for next week:

Rate your week: ___ / 10

monthly review

"Don't ever make a decision based on fear. Make decisions based on hope and possibility. Make decisions based on what should happen, not what shouldn't."

– Michelle Obama

The single biggest/best achievement for the month was:
___
___
___
___

I'm most proud of:
___
___
___
___

My best visualisation strategy was:
___
___
___
___
___

Three things I loved about this month:

1. _____
2. _____
3. _____

My healthiest action was:

My best career move/decision was:

My best mindset practice was:

I felt most successful/enlightened when:

The best moment of courage I had:

A visualisation that came true was:

Three things that didn't go to plan this month:

1. _____
2. _____
3. _____

How I can avoid or improve these things next month:

1. _____
2. _____
3. _____

Three visions and actions I undertook and achieved this month:

1. _____
2. _____
3. _____

> **The universe is always speaking to us — sending us little messages, causing coincidences and serendipities,**

**reminding us to stop. To look around. To believe in something else. Something more.
"**

– Nancy Thayer

DAILY ACCOUNTABILITY

Today's mantra: I will make way for a happy future.

Date: ___ / ___ / _____

Today, I am feeling:

- EXCITED
- STRESSED
- ENERGETIC
- HAPPY
- RELAXED
- RESTED
- SLEEPY
- APATHETIC
- SAD

Daily visualisation

In life: _____

In career: _____

In health/wellness: _____

The BIG goal I'm working towards today:

Today's priorities:

Top three mini goals:

1. _____

2. _____

3. _____

Reflection:

Today's three biggest wins:

1. _____

2. _____

3. _____

DAILY ACCOUNTABILITY

Today's mantra: I am open to new adventures.

Date: ___ /___ /_____

Today, I am feeling:

- EXCITED
- STRESSED
- ENERGETIC
- HAPPY
- RELAXED
- RESTED
- SLEEPY
- APATHETIC
- SAD

Daily visualisation

In life: _____

In career: _____

In health/wellness: _____

The BIG goal I'm working towards today:

Today's priorities:

Top three mini goals:

1. _____

2. _____

3. _____

Reflection:

Today's three biggest wins:

1. _____

2. _____

3. _____

DAILY ACCOUNTABILITY

Today's mantra: I release my fears of not being perfect.

Date: ___ / ___ / _____

Today, I am feeling:

- EXCITED
- STRESSED
- ENERGETIC
- HAPPY
- RELAXED
- RESTED
- SLEEPY
- APATHETIC
- SAD

Daily visualisation

In life: _____

In career: _____

In health/wellness: _____

The BIG goal I'm working towards today:

Today's priorities:

Top three mini goals:

1. _____

2. _____

3. _____

Reflection:

Today's three biggest wins:

1. _____

2. _____

3. _____

DAILY ACCOUNTABILITY

Today's mantra: I know and honour my purpose.

Date: ___ /___ /_____

Today, I am feeling:

- EXCITED
- STRESSED
- ENERGETIC
- HAPPY
- RELAXED
- RESTED
- SLEEPY
- APATHETIC
- SAD

Daily visualisation

In life: _____

In career: _____

In health/wellness: _____

The BIG goal I'm working towards today:

Today's priorities:

Top three mini goals:

1. _____

2. _____

3. _____

Reflection:

Today's three biggest wins:

1. _____

2. _____

3. _____

DAILY ACCOUNTABILITY

Today's mantra: I carry kindness in my heart.

Date: ___ / ___ / _____

Today, I am feeling:

- EXCITED
- HAPPY
- SLEEPY
- STRESSED
- RELAXED
- APATHETIC
- ENERGETIC
- RESTED
- SAD

Daily visualisation

In life: _____

In career: _____

In health/wellness: _____

The BIG goal I'm working towards today:

Today's priorities:

Top three mini goals:

1. _____

2. _____

3. _____

Reflection:

Today's three biggest wins:

1. _____

2. _____

3. _____

DAILY ACCOUNTABILITY

Today's mantra: I am centred and balanced today.

Date: ___ / ___ / _____

Today, I am feeling:

- EXCITED
- HAPPY
- SLEEPY
- STRESSED
- RELAXED
- APATHETIC
- ENERGETIC
- RESTED
- SAD

Daily visualisation

In life: _____

In career: _____

In health/wellness: _____

The BIG goal I'm working towards today:

Today's priorities:

Top three mini goals:

1. _____

2. _____

3. _____

Reflection:

Today's three biggest wins:

1. _____

2. _____

3. _____

DAILY ACCOUNTABILITY

Today's mantra: I will cherish the now, tomorrow and always.

Date: ___ /___ /_____

Today, I am feeling:

- EXCITED
- STRESSED
- ENERGETIC
- HAPPY
- RELAXED
- RESTED
- SLEEPY
- APATHETIC
- SAD

Daily visualisation

In life: _____

In career: _____

In health/wellness: _____

The BIG goal I'm working towards today:

Today's priorities:

Top three mini goals:

1. _____

2. _____

3. _____

Reflection:

Today's three biggest wins:

1. _____

2. _____

3. _____

WEEKLY RECAP

*"The craziest thing is that you think you have time,
when truly there is and only ever will be, now."*

@lisamessenger

Did I complete the past seven days?   Yes ☐   No ☐

If no, why did I miss the day/days: _____

_____

I can do better next week by: _____

_____

My best and/or biggest achievement of the week was:

_____

How is my progress is going towards your big goal?

_____

Reflection:

Some visualisation tools I used this week:

1. _____

2. _____

3. _____

My big actions for next week:

Rate your week: / 10

DAILY ACCOUNTABILITY

Today's mantra: I am privileged to experience life.

Date: ___ / ___ / _____

Today, I am feeling:

- EXCITED
- HAPPY
- SLEEPY
- STRESSED
- RELAXED
- APATHETIC
- ENERGETIC
- RESTED
- SAD

Daily visualisation

In life: _____

In career: _____

In health/wellness: _____

The BIG goal I'm working towards today:

Today's priorities:

Top three mini goals:

1. _____

2. _____

3. _____

Reflection:

Today's three biggest wins:

1. _____

2. _____

3. _____

DAILY ACCOUNTABILITY

Today's mantra: I am walking into my purpose.

Date: ___ /___ /_____

Today, I am feeling:

- EXCITED
- HAPPY
- SLEEPY
- STRESSED
- RELAXED
- APATHETIC
- ENERGETIC
- RESTED
- SAD

Daily visualisation

In life: _____

In career: _____

In health/wellness: _____

> The BIG goal I'm working towards today:

Today's priorities:

Top three mini goals:

1. _____

2. _____

3. _____

Reflection:

Today's three biggest wins:

1. _____

2. _____

3. _____

DAILY ACCOUNTABILITY

Today's mantra: I deserve a life full of joy.

Date: ___ /___ /____

Today, I am feeling:

- EXCITED
- STRESSED
- ENERGETIC
- HAPPY
- RELAXED
- RESTED
- SLEEPY
- APATHETIC
- SAD

Daily visualisation

In life: _____

In career: _____

In health/wellness: _____

The BIG goal I'm working towards today:

Today's priorities:

Top three mini goals:

1. _____

2. _____

3. _____

Reflection:

Today's three biggest wins:

1. _____

2. _____

3. _____

DAILY ACCOUNTABILITY

Today's mantra: Today will be better than yesterday.

Date: ___ /___ /_____

Today, I am feeling:

- EXCITED
- HAPPY
- SLEEPY
- STRESSED
- RELAXED
- APATHETIC
- ENERGETIC
- RESTED
- SAD

Daily visualisation

In life: _____

In career: _____

In health/wellness: _____

> The BIG goal I'm working towards today:

Today's priorities:

Top three mini goals:

1. _____

2. _____

3. _____

Reflection:

Today's three biggest wins:

1. _____

2. _____

3. _____

DAILY ACCOUNTABILITY

Today's mantra: I will better myself every day.

Date: ___ /___ /_____

Today, I am feeling:

- EXCITED
- STRESSED
- ENERGETIC

- HAPPY
- RELAXED
- RESTED

- SLEEPY
- APATHETIC
- SAD

Daily visualisation

In life: _____

In career: _____

In health/wellness: _____

The BIG goal I'm working towards today:

Today's priorities:

Top three mini goals:

1. _____

2. _____

3. _____

Reflection:

Today's three biggest wins:

1. _____

2. _____

3. _____

DAILY ACCOUNTABILITY

Today's mantra: I am scheduling my day to suit me.

Date: ___ /___ /_____

Today, I am feeling:

- EXCITED
- STRESSED
- ENERGETIC
- HAPPY
- RELAXED
- RESTED
- SLEEPY
- APATHETIC
- SAD

Daily visualisation

In life: _____

In career: _____

In health/wellness: _____

> The BIG goal I'm working towards today:

Today's priorities:

Top three mini goals:

1. _____

2. _____

3. _____

Reflection:

Today's three biggest wins:

1. _____

2. _____

3. _____

DAILY ACCOUNTABILITY

Today's mantra: I choose to let go of what no longer serves me.

Date: ___ / ___ / _____

Today, I am feeling:

- EXCITED
- STRESSED
- ENERGETIC
- HAPPY
- RELAXED
- RESTED
- SLEEPY
- APATHETIC
- SAD

Daily visualisation

In life: _____

In career: _____

In health/wellness: _____

The BIG goal I'm working towards today:

Today's priorities:

Top three mini goals:

1. _____

2. _____

3. _____

Reflection:

Today's three biggest wins:

1. _____

2. _____

3. _____

WEEKLY RECAP

"A big, wonderful, fulfilling life is out there and is 100 per cent available to anyone who has the vision, strength and courage to make it so."

@collectivehub

Did I complete the past seven days?   Yes ☐   No ☐

If no, why did I miss the day/days: _____

_____

I can do better next week by: _____

_____

My best and/or biggest achievement of the week was:

_____

How is my progress is going towards your big goal?

_____

Reflection:

Some visualisation tools I used this week:

1. _____

2. _____

3. _____

Rate your week: / 10

My big actions for next week:

DAILY ACCOUNTABILITY

Today's mantra: I will take the time to simply be.

Date: ___ / ___ / _____

Today, I am feeling:

- EXCITED
- STRESSED
- ENERGETIC
- HAPPY
- RELAXED
- RESTED
- SLEEPY
- APATHETIC
- SAD

Daily visualisation

In life: _____

In career: _____

In health/wellness: _____

The BIG goal I'm working towards today:

Today's priorities:

Top three mini goals:

1. _____

2. _____

3. _____

Reflection:

Today's three biggest wins:

1. _____

2. _____

3. _____

DAILY ACCOUNTABILITY

Today's mantra: I belong truly to myself.

Date: ___ /___ /_____

Today, I am feeling:

- EXCITED
- STRESSED
- ENERGETIC
- HAPPY
- RELAXED
- RESTED
- SLEEPY
- APATHETIC
- SAD

Daily visualisation

In life: _____

In career: _____

In health/wellness: _____

The BIG goal I'm working towards today:

Today's priorities:

Top three mini goals:

1. _____

2. _____

3. _____

Reflection:

Today's three biggest wins:

1. _____

2. _____

3. _____

DAILY ACCOUNTABILITY

Today's mantra: I see beauty everywhere.

Date: ___ / ___ / _____

Today, I am feeling:

- EXCITED
- STRESSED
- ENERGETIC
- HAPPY
- RELAXED
- RESTED
- SLEEPY
- APATHETIC
- SAD

Daily visualisation

In life: _____

In career: _____

In health/wellness: _____

The BIG goal I'm working towards today:

Today's priorities:

Top three mini goals:

1. _____

2. _____

3. _____

Reflection:

Today's three biggest wins:

1. _____

2. _____

3. _____

DAILY ACCOUNTABILITY

Today's mantra: I will carve out a life tailored to my wants and whims.

Date: ___ /___ /_____

Today, I am feeling:

- EXCITED
- STRESSED
- ENERGETIC
- HAPPY
- RELAXED
- RESTED
- SLEEPY
- APATHETIC
- SAD

Daily visualisation

In life: _____

In career: _____

In health/wellness: _____

The BIG goal I'm working towards today:

Today's priorities:

Top three mini goals:

1. _____

2. _____

3. _____

Reflection:

Today's three biggest wins:

1. _____

2. _____

3. _____

JOURNALING

DAILY ACCOUNTABILITY

Today's mantra: I will give myself clear and achievable goals.

Date: ___ / ___ / _____

Today, I am feeling:

- EXCITED
- STRESSED
- ENERGETIC
- HAPPY
- RELAXED
- RESTED
- SLEEPY
- APATHETIC
- SAD

Daily visualisation

In life: _____

In career: _____

In health/wellness: _____

The BIG goal I'm working towards today:

Today's priorities:

Top three mini goals:

1. _____

2. _____

3. _____

Reflection:

Today's three biggest wins:

1. _____

2. _____

3. _____

DAILY ACCOUNTABILITY

Today's mantra: I will allow my body to go where it wants to go.

Date: ___ /___ /_____

Today, I am feeling:

- EXCITED
- STRESSED
- ENERGETIC

- HAPPY
- RELAXED
- RESTED

- SLEEPY
- APATHETIC
- SAD

Daily visualisation

In life: _____

In career: _____

In health/wellness: _____

The BIG goal I'm working towards today:

Today's priorities:

Top three mini goals:

1. _____

2. _____

3. _____

Reflection:

Today's three biggest wins:

1. _____

2. _____

3. _____

DAILY ACCOUNTABILITY

Today's mantra: I will positively move my body today.

Date: ___ / ___ / _____

Today, I am feeling:

- EXCITED
- STRESSED
- ENERGETIC
- HAPPY
- RELAXED
- RESTED
- SLEEPY
- APATHETIC
- SAD

Daily visualisation

In life: _____

In career: _____

In health/wellness: _____

> The BIG goal I'm working towards today:

Today's priorities:

Top three mini goals:

1. _____

2. _____

3. _____

Reflection:

Today's three biggest wins:

1. _____

2. _____

3. _____

WEEKLY RECAP

*"True belonging doesn't require you to change who you are.
It requires you to be who you are."*

– Brené Brown

Did I complete the past seven days?   Yes ☐   No ☐

If no, why did I miss the day/days: _____

_____

I can do better next week by: _____

_____

My best and/or biggest achievement of the week was:

_____

How is my progress is going towards your big goal?

_____

Reflection:

Some visualisation tools I used this week:

1. _____

2. _____

3. _____

My big actions for next week:

Rate your week: / 10

DAILY ACCOUNTABILITY

Today's mantra: I will risk it all for my dreams.

Date: ___ / ___ / ____

Today, I am feeling:

- EXCITED
- STRESSED
- ENERGETIC
- HAPPY
- RELAXED
- RESTED
- SLEEPY
- APATHETIC
- SAD

Daily visualisation

In life: _____

In career: _____

In health/wellness: _____

The BIG goal I'm working towards today:

Today's priorities:

Top three mini goals:

1. _____

2. _____

3. _____

Reflection:

Today's three biggest wins:

1. _____

2. _____

3. _____

DAILY ACCOUNTABILITY

Today's mantra: I believe in the alignment of the universe.

Date: ___ / ___ / _____

Today, I am feeling:

- EXCITED
- HAPPY
- SLEEPY
- STRESSED
- RELAXED
- APATHETIC
- ENERGETIC
- RESTED
- SAD

Daily visualisation

In life: _____

In career: _____

In health/wellness: _____

The BIG goal I'm working towards today:

Today's priorities:

Top three mini goals:

1. _____

2. _____

3. _____

Reflection:

Today's three biggest wins:

1. _____

2. _____

3. _____

DAILY ACCOUNTABILITY

Today's mantra: I give power to myself.

Date: ___ / ___ / _____

Today, I am feeling:

- EXCITED
- STRESSED
- ENERGETIC
- HAPPY
- RELAXED
- RESTED
- SLEEPY
- APATHETIC
- SAD

Daily visualisation

In life: _____

In career: _____

In health/wellness: _____

The BIG goal I'm working towards today:

Today's priorities:

Top three mini goals:

1. _____

2. _____

3. _____

Reflection:

Today's three biggest wins:

1. _____

2. _____

3. _____

DAILY ACCOUNTABILITY

Today's mantra: I am grateful for the good that surrounds me.

Date: ___ / ___ / _____

Today, I am feeling:

- EXCITED
- STRESSED
- ENERGETIC
- HAPPY
- RELAXED
- RESTED
- SLEEPY
- APATHETIC
- SAD

Daily visualisation

In life: _____

In career: _____

In health/wellness: _____

The BIG goal I'm working towards today:

Today's priorities:

Top three mini goals:

1. _____

2. _____

3. _____

Reflection:

Today's three biggest wins:

1. _____

2. _____

3. _____

DAILY ACCOUNTABILITY

Today's mantra: I will be relentless in my pursuit of passion.

Date: ___ /___ /_____

Today, I am feeling:

- EXCITED
- STRESSED
- ENERGETIC
- HAPPY
- RELAXED
- RESTED
- SLEEPY
- APATHETIC
- SAD

Daily visualisation

In life: _____

In career: _____

In health/wellness: _____

The BIG goal I'm working towards today:

Today's priorities:

Top three mini goals:

1. _____

2. _____

3. _____

Reflection:

Today's three biggest wins:

1. _____

2. _____

3. _____

DAILY ACCOUNTABILITY

Today's mantra: I am centred.

Date: ___ /___ /____

Today, I am feeling:

- EXCITED
- STRESSED
- ENERGETIC
- HAPPY
- RELAXED
- RESTED
- SLEEPY
- APATHETIC
- SAD

Daily visualisation

In life: _____

In career: _____

In health/wellness: _____

The BIG goal I'm working towards today:

Today's priorities:

Top three mini goals:

1. _____

2. _____

3. _____

Reflection:

Today's three biggest wins:

1. _____

2. _____

3. _____

DAILY ACCOUNTABILITY

Today's mantra: I choose to live life at a comfortable pace.

Date: ___ / ___ / _____

Today, I am feeling:

- EXCITED
- STRESSED
- ENERGETIC
- HAPPY
- RELAXED
- RESTED
- SLEEPY
- APATHETIC
- SAD

Daily visualisation

In life: _____

In career: _____

In health/wellness: _____

The BIG goal I'm working towards today:

Today's priorities:

Top three mini goals:

1. _____

2. _____

3. _____

Reflection:

Today's three biggest wins:

1. _____

2. _____

3. _____

WEEKLY RECAP

"People say 'Go big or go home' as if going home were a bad thing.
Hell yeah, I wanna go home.
And I'm going to take a nap when I get there."

– Anon

Did I complete the past seven days?   Yes ☐   No ☐

If no, why did I miss the day/days: _____

_____

I can do better next week by: _____

_____

My best and/or biggest achievement of the week was:

_____

How is my progress is going towards your big goal?

_____

Reflection:

Some visualisation tools I used this week:

1. _____

2. _____

3. _____

My big actions for next week:

Rate your week: /10

monthly review

"The older you get, the more you realise that it isn't about the material things, or pride or ego. It's about our hearts and who they beat for."

– J. Sterling

The single biggest/best achievement for the month was:
_____
_____
_____

I'm most proud of:
_____
_____
_____
_____

My best visualisation strategy was:
_____
_____
_____
_____
_____

Three things I loved about this month:

1. _____
2. _____
3. _____

My healthiest action was:

My best career move/decision was:

My best mindset practice was:

I felt most successful/enlightened when:

The best moment of courage I had:

A visualisation that came true was:

Three things that didn't go to plan this month:

1. _____
2. _____
3. _____

How I can avoid or improve these things next month:

1. _____
2. _____
3. _____

Three visions and actions I undertook and achieved this month:

1. _____
2. _____
3. _____

> **If you don't have a vision, you're going to be stuck in what you know.**

And the only thing you know is what you've already seen.

"

– Iyanla Vanzant

DAILY ACCOUNTABILITY

Today's mantra: I will face my challenges head-on.

Date: ___ / ___ / _____

Today, I am feeling:

- EXCITED
- STRESSED
- ENERGETIC
- HAPPY
- RELAXED
- RESTED
- SLEEPY
- APATHETIC
- SAD

Daily visualisation

In life: _____

In career: _____

In health/wellness: _____

The BIG goal I'm working towards today:

Today's priorities:

Top three mini goals:

1. _____

2. _____

3. _____

Reflection:

Today's three biggest wins:

1. _____

2. _____

3. _____

VISIONS & ACTIONS

DAILY ACCOUNTABILITY

Today's mantra: I accept myself and I feel great about myself.

Date: ___ / ___ / _____

Today, I am feeling:

- EXCITED
- STRESSED
- ENERGETIC
- HAPPY
- RELAXED
- RESTED
- SLEEPY
- APATHETIC
- SAD

Daily visualisation

In life: _____

In career: _____

In health/wellness: _____

The BIG goal I'm working towards today:

Today's priorities:

Top three mini goals:

1. _____

2. _____

3. _____

Reflection:

Today's three biggest wins:

1. _____

2. _____

3. _____

DAILY ACCOUNTABILITY

Today's mantra: I will consider my responses and actions.

Date: ___ / ___ / _____

Today, I am feeling:

- EXCITED
- STRESSED
- ENERGETIC
- HAPPY
- RELAXED
- RESTED
- SLEEPY
- APATHETIC
- SAD

Daily visualisation

In life: _____

In career: _____

In health/wellness: _____

The BIG goal I'm working towards today:

Today's priorities:

Top three mini goals:

1. _____

2. _____

3. _____

Reflection:

Today's three biggest wins:

1. _____

2. _____

3. _____

DAILY ACCOUNTABILITY

Today's mantra: I am worthy.

Date: ___ / ___ / _____

Today, I am feeling:

- EXCITED
- STRESSED
- ENERGETIC
- HAPPY
- RELAXED
- RESTED
- SLEEPY
- APATHETIC
- SAD

Daily visualisation

In life: _____

In career: _____

In health/wellness: _____

```
The BIG goal I'm working towards today:



```

Today's priorities:

Top three mini goals:

1. _____

2. _____

3. _____

Reflection:

Today's three biggest wins:

1. _____

2. _____

3. _____

DAILY ACCOUNTABILITY

Today's mantra: I won't be afraid to close the door and open another.

Date: ___ /___ /____

Today, I am feeling:

- EXCITED
- STRESSED
- ENERGETIC
- HAPPY
- RELAXED
- RESTED
- SLEEPY
- APATHETIC
- SAD

Daily visualisation

In life: _____

In career: _____

In health/wellness: _____

The BIG goal I'm working towards today:

Today's priorities:

Top three mini goals:

1. _____

2. _____

3. _____

Reflection:

Today's three biggest wins:

1. _____

2. _____

3. _____

VISIONS & ACTIONS

DAILY ACCOUNTABILITY

Today's mantra: I am aware of my desires and intend to pursue them.

Date: ___ /___ /_____

Today, I am feeling:

- EXCITED
- HAPPY
- SLEEPY
- STRESSED
- RELAXED
- APATHETIC
- ENERGETIC
- RESTED
- SAD

Daily visualisation

In life: _____

In career: _____

In health/wellness: _____

The BIG goal I'm working towards today:

Today's priorities:

Top three mini goals:

1. _____

2. _____

3. _____

Reflection:

Today's three biggest wins:

1. _____

2. _____

3. _____

DAILY ACCOUNTABILITY

Today's mantra: I am open to new possibilities.

Date: ___ /___ /_____

Today, I am feeling:

- EXCITED
- STRESSED
- ENERGETIC
- HAPPY
- RELAXED
- RESTED
- SLEEPY
- APATHETIC
- SAD

Daily visualisation

In life: _____

In career: _____

In health/wellness: _____

The BIG goal I'm working towards today:

Today's priorities:

Top three mini goals:

1. _____

2. _____

3. _____

Reflection:

Today's three biggest wins:

1. _____

2. _____

3. _____

WEEKLY RECAP

"Maybe the journey isn't so much about becoming anything. Maybe it's about unbecoming everything that isn't really you so that you can be who you were meant to be in the first place."

– Paulo Coelho

Did I complete the past seven days?   Yes ☐   No ☐

If no, why did I miss the day/days: _____

_____

I can do better next week by: _____

_____

My best and/or biggest achievement of the week was:

_____

How is my progress is going towards your big goal?

_____

Reflection:

Some visualisation tools I used this week:

1. _____

2. _____

3. _____

My big actions for next week:

Rate your week: ___ / 10

DAILY ACCOUNTABILITY

Today's mantra: I will lighten the burden of others.

Date: ___ / ___ / ____

Today, I am feeling:

- EXCITED
- STRESSED
- ENERGETIC
- HAPPY
- RELAXED
- RESTED
- SLEEPY
- APATHETIC
- SAD

Daily visualisation

In life: _____

In career: _____

In health/wellness: _____

The BIG goal I'm working towards today:

Today's priorities:

Top three mini goals:

1. _____

2. _____

3. _____

Reflection:

Today's three biggest wins:

1. _____

2. _____

3. _____

DAILY ACCOUNTABILITY

Today's mantra: Today, I will give back.

Date: ___ /___ /_____

Today, I am feeling:

- EXCITED
- STRESSED
- ENERGETIC
- HAPPY
- RELAXED
- RESTED
- SLEEPY
- APATHETIC
- SAD

Daily visualisation

In life: _____

In career: _____

In health/wellness: _____

The BIG goal I'm working towards today:

Today's priorities:

Top three mini goals:

1. _____

2. _____

3. _____

Reflection:

Today's three biggest wins:

1. _____

2. _____

3. _____

DAILY ACCOUNTABILITY

Today's mantra: I will try something new today.

Date: ___ /___ /____

Today, I am feeling:

- EXCITED
- STRESSED
- ENERGETIC

- HAPPY
- RELAXED
- RESTED

- SLEEPY
- APATHETIC
- SAD

Daily visualisation

In life: _____

In career: _____

In health/wellness: _____

The BIG goal I'm working towards today:

Today's priorities:

Top three mini goals:

1. _____

2. _____

3. _____

Reflection:

Today's three biggest wins:

1. _____

2. _____

3. _____

DAILY ACCOUNTABILITY

Today's mantra: I am enjoying the journey.

Date: ___ /___ /_____

Today, I am feeling:

- EXCITED
- STRESSED
- ENERGETIC
- HAPPY
- RELAXED
- RESTED
- SLEEPY
- APATHETIC
- SAD

Daily visualisation

In life: _____

In career: _____

In health/wellness: _____

```
The BIG goal I'm working towards today:
```

Today's priorities:

Top three mini goals:

1. _____

2. _____

3. _____

Reflection:

Today's three biggest wins:

1. _____

2. _____

3. _____

DAILY ACCOUNTABILITY

Today's mantra: I love and embrace my imperfections.

Date: ___ / ___ / _____

Today, I am feeling:

- EXCITED
- STRESSED
- ENERGETIC
- HAPPY
- RELAXED
- RESTED
- SLEEPY
- APATHETIC
- SAD

Daily visualisation

In life: _____

In career: _____

In health/wellness: _____

The BIG goal I'm working towards today:

Today's priorities:

Top three mini goals:

1. _____

2. _____

3. _____

Reflection:

Today's three biggest wins:

1. _____

2. _____

3. _____

DAILY ACCOUNTABILITY

Today's mantra: I am strong, courageous and live life to the fullest.

Date: ___ / ___ / _____

Today, I am feeling:

- EXCITED
- STRESSED
- ENERGETIC
- HAPPY
- RELAXED
- RESTED
- SLEEPY
- APATHETIC
- SAD

Daily visualisation

In life: _____

In career: _____

In health/wellness: _____

The BIG goal I'm working towards today:

Today's priorities:

Top three mini goals:

1. _____

2. _____

3. _____

Reflection:

Today's three biggest wins:

1. _____

2. _____

3. _____

DAILY ACCOUNTABILITY

Today's mantra: I will let my heart lead the way.

Date: ___ / ___ / _____

Today, I am feeling:

- EXCITED
- STRESSED
- ENERGETIC
- HAPPY
- RELAXED
- RESTED
- SLEEPY
- APATHETIC
- SAD

Daily visualisation

In life: _____

In career: _____

In health/wellness: _____

The BIG goal I'm working towards today:

Today's priorities:

Top three mini goals:

1. _____

2. _____

3. _____

Reflection:

Today's three biggest wins:

1. _____

2. _____

3. _____

WEEKLY RECAP

*"The one thing you have that nobody else has is you.
Your voice, your vision. So write and draw and build
and play and dance and live as only you can."*

– Neil Gaiman

Did I complete the past seven days?   Yes ☐   No ☐

If no, why did I miss the day/days: _____

_____

I can do better next week by: _____

_____

My best and/or biggest achievement of the week was:

_____

How is my progress is going towards your big goal?

_____

Reflection:

Some visualisation tools I used this week:

1. _____

2. _____

3. _____

Rate your week: / 10

My big actions for next week:

DAILY ACCOUNTABILITY

Today's mantra: The path ahead is the right one.

Date: ___ / ___ / _____

Today, I am feeling:

- EXCITED
- STRESSED
- ENERGETIC
- HAPPY
- RELAXED
- RESTED
- SLEEPY
- APATHETIC
- SAD

Daily visualisation

In life: _____

In career: _____

In health/wellness: _____

The BIG goal I'm working towards today:

Today's priorities:

Top three mini goals:

1. _____

2. _____

3. _____

Reflection:

Today's three biggest wins:

1. _____

2. _____

3. _____

DAILY ACCOUNTABILITY

Today's mantra: I love everyone in my life right now.

Date: ___ / ___ / _____

Today, I am feeling:

- EXCITED
- STRESSED
- ENERGETIC
- HAPPY
- RELAXED
- RESTED
- SLEEPY
- APATHETIC
- SAD

Daily visualisation

In life: _____

In career: _____

In health/wellness: _____

The BIG goal I'm working towards today:

Today's priorities:

Top three mini goals:

1. _____

2. _____

3. _____

Reflection:

Today's three biggest wins:

1. _____

2. _____

3. _____

JOURNALING

DAILY ACCOUNTABILITY

Today's mantra: I am enjoying my own pace of life.

Date: ___ / ___ / _____

Today, I am feeling:

- EXCITED
- STRESSED
- ENERGETIC
- HAPPY
- RELAXED
- RESTED
- SLEEPY
- APATHETIC
- SAD

Daily visualisation

In life: _____

In career: _____

In health/wellness: _____

The BIG goal I'm working towards today:

Today's priorities:

Top three mini goals:

1. _____

2. _____

3. _____

Reflection:

Today's three biggest wins:

1. _____

2. _____

3. _____

DAILY ACCOUNTABILITY

Today's mantra: I will break an old habit.

Date: ___ /___ /_____

Today, I am feeling:

- EXCITED
- STRESSED
- ENERGETIC
- HAPPY
- RELAXED
- RESTED
- SLEEPY
- APATHETIC
- SAD

Daily visualisation

In life: _____

In career: _____

In health/wellness: _____

The BIG goal I'm working towards today:

Today's priorities:

Top three mini goals:

1. _____

2. _____

3. _____

Reflection:

Today's three biggest wins:

1. _____

2. _____

3. _____

DAILY ACCOUNTABILITY

Today's mantra: I will stop ignoring myself and my body.

Date: ___ / ___ / _____

Today, I am feeling:

- EXCITED
- STRESSED
- ENERGETIC
- HAPPY
- RELAXED
- RESTED
- SLEEPY
- APATHETIC
- SAD

Daily visualisation

In life: _____

In career: _____

In health/wellness: _____

The BIG goal I'm working towards today:

Today's priorities:

Top three mini goals:

1. _____

2. _____

3. _____

Reflection:

Today's three biggest wins:

1. _____

2. _____

3. _____

DAILY ACCOUNTABILITY

Today's mantra: I am letting go of the bad to make way for the great.

Date: ___ / ___ / _____

Today, I am feeling:

- EXCITED
- HAPPY
- SLEEPY
- STRESSED
- RELAXED
- APATHETIC
- ENERGETIC
- RESTED
- SAD

Daily visualisation

In life: _____

In career: _____

In health/wellness: _____

The BIG goal I'm working towards today:

Today's priorities:

Top three mini goals:

1. _____

2. _____

3. _____

Reflection:

Today's three biggest wins:

1. _____

2. _____

3. _____

DAILY ACCOUNTABILITY

Today's mantra: I will undertake a new challenge.

Date: ___ / ___ / _____

Today, I am feeling:

- EXCITED
- STRESSED
- ENERGETIC
- HAPPY
- RELAXED
- RESTED
- SLEEPY
- APATHETIC
- SAD

Daily visualisation

In life: _____

In career: _____

In health/wellness: _____

The BIG goal I'm working towards today:

Today's priorities:

Top three mini goals:

1. _____

2. _____

3. _____

Reflection:

Today's three biggest wins:

1. _____

2. _____

3. _____

WEEKLY RECAP

"You don't need to be perfect to inspire others. Let people be inspired by how you deal with your imperfections."

– Ziad K Abdelnour

Did I complete the past seven days?   Yes ☐   No ☐

If no, why did I miss the day/days: _____

_____

I can do better next week by: _____

_____

My best and/or biggest achievement of the week was:

_____

How is my progress is going towards your big goal?

_____

Reflection:

Some visualisation tools I used this week:

1. _____

2. _____

3. _____

My big actions for next week:

Rate your week: /10

DAILY ACCOUNTABILITY

Today's mantra: I will be focused on getting things done.

Date: ___ /___ /_____

Today, I am feeling:

- EXCITED
- STRESSED
- ENERGETIC
- HAPPY
- RELAXED
- RESTED
- SLEEPY
- APATHETIC
- SAD

Daily visualisation

In life: _____

In career: _____

In health/wellness: _____

The BIG goal I'm working towards today:

Today's priorities:

Top three mini goals:

1. _____

2. _____

3. _____

Reflection:

Today's three biggest wins:

1. _____

2. _____

3. _____

DAILY ACCOUNTABILITY

Today's mantra: I will trust the process.

Date: ___ / ___ / _____

Today, I am feeling:

- EXCITED
- STRESSED
- ENERGETIC
- HAPPY
- RELAXED
- RESTED
- SLEEPY
- APATHETIC
- SAD

Daily visualisation

In life: _____

In career: _____

In health/wellness: _____

The BIG goal I'm working towards today:

Today's priorities:

Top three mini goals:

1. _____

2. _____

3. _____

Reflection:

Today's three biggest wins:

1. _____

2. _____

3. _____

DAILY ACCOUNTABILITY

Today's mantra: I will embrace whatever is coming my way.

Date: ___ / ___ / _____

Today, I am feeling:

- EXCITED
- STRESSED
- ENERGETIC
- HAPPY
- RELAXED
- RESTED
- SLEEPY
- APATHETIC
- SAD

Daily visualisation

In life: _____

In career: _____

In health/wellness: _____

The BIG goal I'm working towards today:

Today's priorities:

Top three mini goals:

1. _____

2. _____

3. _____

Reflection:

Today's three biggest wins:

1. _____

2. _____

3. _____

DAILY ACCOUNTABILITY

Today's mantra: I celebrate all that is right in this world.

Date: ___ /___ /_____

Today, I am feeling:

- EXCITED
- STRESSED
- ENERGETIC
- HAPPY
- RELAXED
- RESTED
- SLEEPY
- APATHETIC
- SAD

Daily visualisation

In life: _____

In career: _____

In health/wellness: _____

The BIG goal I'm working towards today:

Today's priorities:

Top three mini goals:

1. _____

2. _____

3. _____

Reflection:

Today's three biggest wins:

1. _____

2. _____

3. _____

DAILY ACCOUNTABILITY

Today's mantra: I will push my excuses away.

Date: ___ / ___ / ____

Today, I am feeling:

- EXCITED
- STRESSED
- ENERGETIC
- HAPPY
- RELAXED
- RESTED
- SLEEPY
- APATHETIC
- SAD

Daily visualisation

In life: _____

In career: _____

In health/wellness: _____

```
The BIG goal I'm working towards today:


```

Today's priorities:

Top three mini goals:

1. _____

2. _____

3. _____

Reflection:

Today's three biggest wins:

1. _____

2. _____

3. _____

DAILY ACCOUNTABILITY

Today's mantra: I am brave enough to ask for what I want.

Date: ___ /___ /_____

Today, I am feeling:

- EXCITED
- STRESSED
- ENERGETIC
- HAPPY
- RELAXED
- RESTED
- SLEEPY
- APATHETIC
- SAD

Daily visualisation

In life: _____

In career: _____

In health/wellness: _____

The BIG goal I'm working towards today:

Today's priorities:

Top three mini goals:

1. _____

2. _____

3. _____

Reflection:

Today's three biggest wins:

1. _____

2. _____

3. _____

DAILY ACCOUNTABILITY

Today's mantra: I am embracing silence.

Date: ___ / ___ / _____

Today, I am feeling:

- EXCITED
- STRESSED
- ENERGETIC
- HAPPY
- RELAXED
- RESTED
- SLEEPY
- APATHETIC
- SAD

Daily visualisation

In life: _____

In career: _____

In health/wellness: _____

```
The BIG goal I'm working towards today:


```

Today's priorities:

Top three mini goals:

1. _____

2. _____

3. _____

Reflection:

Today's three biggest wins:

1. _____

2. _____

3. _____

WEEKLY RECAP

*"Set your agenda each day or the world will do it for you.
Don't decide on your next move based on the demands of
your inbox but on the direction of your dreams."*

– Brendon Burchard

Did I complete the past seven days?   Yes ☐   No ☐

If no, why did I miss the day/days: _____

_____

I can do better next week by: _____

_____

My best and/or biggest achievement of the week was:

_____

How is my progress is going towards your big goal?

_____

Reflection:

Some visualisation tools I used this week:

1. _____

2. _____

3. _____

Rate your week: /10

My big actions for next week:

monthly review

"Sometimes crying is the strongest, bravest and most cathartic thing we can do. Be unafraid to let it flow. Feel everything deeply."

@lisamessenger

The single biggest/best achievement for the month was:
_____
_____
_____
_____

I'm most proud of:
_____
_____
_____
_____

My best visualisation strategy was:
_____
_____
_____
_____
_____

Three things I loved about this month:

1. _____
2. _____
3. _____

My healthiest action was:

My best career move/decision was:

My best mindset practice was:

I felt most successful/enlightened when:

The best moment of courage I had:

A visualisation that came true was:

Three things that didn't go to plan this month:

1. _____
2. _____
3. _____

How I can avoid or improve these things next month:

1. _____
2. _____
3. _____

Three visions and actions I undertook and achieved this month:

1. _____
2. _____
3. _____

> Challenges are gifts that force us to search for a new centre of gravity.

Don't fight them. Just find a new way to stand.
"

– Oprah Winfrey

DAILY ACCOUNTABILITY

Today's mantra: I will see challenges as gifts to learn.

Date: ___ /___ /_____

Today, I am feeling:

- EXCITED
- STRESSED
- ENERGETIC
- HAPPY
- RELAXED
- RESTED
- SLEEPY
- APATHETIC
- SAD

Daily visualisation

In life: _____

In career: _____

In health/wellness: _____

The BIG goal I'm working towards today:

Today's priorities:

Top three mini goals:

1. _____

2. _____

3. _____

Reflection:

Today's three biggest wins:

1. _____

2. _____

3. _____

DAILY ACCOUNTABILITY

Today's mantra: Today is a beautiful day.

Date: ___ /___ /_____

Today, I am feeling:

- EXCITED
- HAPPY
- SLEEPY
- STRESSED
- RELAXED
- APATHETIC
- ENERGETIC
- RESTED
- SAD

Daily visualisation

In life: _____

In career: _____

In health/wellness: _____

The BIG goal I'm working towards today:

Today's priorities:

Top three mini goals:

1. _____

2. _____

3. _____

Reflection:

Today's three biggest wins:

1. _____

2. _____

3. _____

DAILY ACCOUNTABILITY

Today's mantra: I am strong.

Date: ___ / ___ / ____

Today, I am feeling:

- EXCITED
- HAPPY
- SLEEPY
- STRESSED
- RELAXED
- APATHETIC
- ENERGETIC
- RESTED
- SAD

Daily visualisation

In life: _____

In career: _____

In health/wellness: _____

The BIG goal I'm working towards today:

Today's priorities:

Top three mini goals:

1. _____

2. _____

3. _____

Reflection:

Today's three biggest wins:

1. _____

2. _____

3. _____

DAILY ACCOUNTABILITY

Today's mantra: I am wishing well for someone in need.

Date: ___ / ___ / _____

Today, I am feeling:

- EXCITED
- STRESSED
- ENERGETIC
- HAPPY
- RELAXED
- RESTED
- SLEEPY
- APATHETIC
- SAD

Daily visualisation

In life: _____

In career: _____

In health/wellness: _____

The BIG goal I'm working towards today:

Today's priorities:

Top three mini goals:

1. _____

2. _____

3. _____

Reflection:

Today's three biggest wins:

1. _____

2. _____

3. _____

DAILY ACCOUNTABILITY

Today's mantra: I am mindful in every moment.

Date: ___ /___ /_____

Today, I am feeling:

- EXCITED
- STRESSED
- ENERGETIC
- HAPPY
- RELAXED
- RESTED
- SLEEPY
- APATHETIC
- SAD

Daily visualisation

In life: _____

In career: _____

In health/wellness: _____

The BIG goal I'm working towards today:

Today's priorities:

Top three mini goals:

1. _____

2. _____

3. _____

Reflection:

Today's three biggest wins:

1. _____

2. _____

3. _____

DAILY ACCOUNTABILITY

Today's mantra: I am proud of my achievements.

Date: ___ /___ /_____

Today, I am feeling:

- EXCITED
- STRESSED
- ENERGETIC
- HAPPY
- RELAXED
- RESTED
- SLEEPY
- APATHETIC
- SAD

Daily visualisation

In life: _____

In career: _____

In health/wellness: _____

The BIG goal I'm working towards today:

Today's priorities:

Top three mini goals:

1. _____

2. _____

3. _____

Reflection:

Today's three biggest wins:

1. _____

2. _____

3. _____

DAILY ACCOUNTABILITY

Today's mantra: I am in control of my life.

Date: ___ / ___ / _____

Today, I am feeling:

- EXCITED
- STRESSED
- ENERGETIC
- HAPPY
- RELAXED
- RESTED
- SLEEPY
- APATHETIC
- SAD

Daily visualisation

In life: _____

In career: _____

In health/wellness: _____

The BIG goal I'm working towards today:

Today's priorities:

Top three mini goals:

1. _____

2. _____

3. _____

Reflection:

Today's three biggest wins:

1. _____

2. _____

3. _____

WEEKLY RECAP

"When one door of happiness closes, another opens; but often we look so long at the closed door that we do not see the one which has been opened for us."

– Helen Keller

Did I complete the past seven days? Yes ☐   No ☐

If no, why did I miss the day/days: _____

_____

I can do better next week by: _____

_____

My best and/or biggest achievement of the week was:

_____

How is my progress is going towards your big goal?

_____

Reflection:

Some visualisation tools I used this week:

1. _____

2. _____

3. _____

My big actions for next week:

Rate your week: ___ / 10

DAILY ACCOUNTABILITY

Today's mantra: I will offer a hand to those who need it.

Date: ___ / ___ / _____

Today, I am feeling:

- EXCITED
- STRESSED
- ENERGETIC
- HAPPY
- RELAXED
- RESTED
- SLEEPY
- APATHETIC
- SAD

Daily visualisation

In life: _____

In career: _____

In health/wellness: _____

The BIG goal I'm working towards today:

Today's priorities:

Top three mini goals:

1. _____

2. _____

3. _____

Reflection:

Today's three biggest wins:

1. _____

2. _____

3. _____

DAILY ACCOUNTABILITY

Today's mantra: I will send kindness into the universe.

Date: ___ /___ /_____

Today, I am feeling:

- EXCITED
- STRESSED
- ENERGETIC
- HAPPY
- RELAXED
- RESTED
- SLEEPY
- APATHETIC
- SAD

Daily visualisation

In life: _____

In career: _____

In health/wellness: _____

The BIG goal I'm working towards today:

Today's priorities:

Top three mini goals:

1. _____

2. _____

3. _____

Reflection:

Today's three biggest wins:

1. _____

2. _____

3. _____

DAILY ACCOUNTABILITY

Today's mantra: I breathe in good thoughts.

Date: ___ / ___ / _____

Today, I am feeling:

- EXCITED
- STRESSED
- ENERGETIC
- HAPPY
- RELAXED
- RESTED
- SLEEPY
- APATHETIC
- SAD

Daily visualisation

In life: _____

In career: _____

In health/wellness: _____

The BIG goal I'm working towards today:

Today's priorities:

Top three mini goals:

1. _____

2. _____

3. _____

Reflection:

Today's three biggest wins:

1. _____

2. _____

3. _____

VISIONS & ACTIONS

DAILY ACCOUNTABILITY

Today's mantra: I will reward my body with what it deserves.

Date: ___ / ___ / _____

Today, I am feeling:

- EXCITED
- STRESSED
- ENERGETIC
- HAPPY
- RELAXED
- RESTED
- SLEEPY
- APATHETIC
- SAD

Daily visualisation

In life: _____

In career: _____

In health/wellness: _____

The BIG goal I'm working towards today:

Today's priorities:

Top three mini goals:

1. _____

2. _____

3. _____

Reflection:

Today's three biggest wins:

1. _____

2. _____

3. _____

DAILY ACCOUNTABILITY

Today's mantra: I release my past.

Date: ___ /___ /_____

Today, I am feeling:

- EXCITED
- STRESSED
- ENERGETIC
- HAPPY
- RELAXED
- RESTED
- SLEEPY
- APATHETIC
- SAD

Daily visualisation

In life: _____

In career: _____

In health/wellness: _____

The BIG goal I'm working towards today:

Today's priorities:

Top three mini goals:

1. _____

2. _____

3. _____

Reflection:

Today's three biggest wins:

1. _____

2. _____

3. _____

DAILY ACCOUNTABILITY

Today's mantra: I will let go of all my anxieties and trust the process.

Date: ___ /___ /_____

Today, I am feeling:

- EXCITED
- STRESSED
- ENERGETIC
- HAPPY
- RELAXED
- RESTED
- SLEEPY
- APATHETIC
- SAD

Daily visualisation

In life: _____

In career: _____

In health/wellness: _____

```
The BIG goal I'm working towards today:



```

Today's priorities:

Top three mini goals:

1. _____

2. _____

3. _____

Reflection:

Today's three biggest wins:

1. _____

2. _____

3. _____

DAILY ACCOUNTABILITY

Today's mantra: I will start fresh!

Date: ___ / ___ / _____

Today, I am feeling:

- EXCITED
- STRESSED
- ENERGETIC
- HAPPY
- RELAXED
- RESTED
- SLEEPY
- APATHETIC
- SAD

Daily visualisation

In life: _____

In career: _____

In health/wellness: _____

The BIG goal I'm working towards today:

Today's priorities:

Top three mini goals:

1. _____

2. _____

3. _____

Reflection:

Today's three biggest wins:

1. _____

2. _____

3. _____

WEEKLY RECAP

"I've never seen any life transformation that didn't begin with the person in question finally getting tired of their own bullsh*t."

– Elizabeth Gilbert

Did I complete the past seven days?   Yes ☐   No ☐

If no, why did I miss the day/days: _____

_____

I can do better next week by: _____

_____

My best and/or biggest achievement of the week was:

_____

How is my progress is going towards your big goal?

_____

Reflection:

Some visualisation tools I used this week:

1. _____

2. _____

3. _____

Rate your week: /10

My big actions for next week:

DAILY ACCOUNTABILITY

Today's mantra: I will say no to anything that doesn't feel right.

Date: ___ / ___ / _____

Today, I am feeling:

- EXCITED
- STRESSED
- ENERGETIC
- HAPPY
- RELAXED
- RESTED
- SLEEPY
- APATHETIC
- SAD

Daily visualisation

In life: _____

In career: _____

In health/wellness: _____

The BIG goal I'm working towards today:

Today's priorities:

Top three mini goals:

1. _____

2. _____

3. _____

Reflection:

Today's three biggest wins:

1. _____

2. _____

3. _____

DAILY ACCOUNTABILITY

Today's mantra: I will practise the path of less clutter.

Date: ___ /___ /_____

Today, I am feeling:

- EXCITED
- HAPPY
- SLEEPY
- STRESSED
- RELAXED
- APATHETIC
- ENERGETIC
- RESTED
- SAD

Daily visualisation

In life: _____

In career: _____

In health/wellness: _____

The BIG goal I'm working towards today:

Today's priorities:

Top three mini goals:

1. _____

2. _____

3. _____

Reflection:

Today's three biggest wins:

1. _____

2. _____

3. _____

DAILY ACCOUNTABILITY

Today's mantra: I am clearing my mind for bigger and better things.

Date: ___ / ___ / _____

Today, I am feeling:

- EXCITED
- STRESSED
- ENERGETIC
- HAPPY
- RELAXED
- RESTED
- SLEEPY
- APATHETIC
- SAD

Daily visualisation

In life: _____

In career: _____

In health/wellness: _____

The BIG goal I'm working towards today:

Today's priorities:

Top three mini goals:

1. _____

2. _____

3. _____

Reflection:

Today's three biggest wins:

1. _____

2. _____

3. _____

DAILY ACCOUNTABILITY

Today's mantra: I will speak up about things I care about.

Date: ___ /___ /_____

Today, I am feeling:

- EXCITED
- STRESSED
- ENERGETIC
- HAPPY
- RELAXED
- RESTED
- SLEEPY
- APATHETIC
- SAD

Daily visualisation

In life: _____

In career: _____

In health/wellness: _____

The BIG goal I'm working towards today:

Today's priorities:

Top three mini goals:

1. _____

2. _____

3. _____

Reflection:

Today's three biggest wins:

1. _____

2. _____

3. _____

DAILY ACCOUNTABILITY

Today's mantra: I will step out of my comfort zone.

Date: ___ / ___ / _____

Today, I am feeling:

- EXCITED
- HAPPY
- SLEEPY
- STRESSED
- RELAXED
- APATHETIC
- ENERGETIC
- RESTED
- SAD

Daily visualisation

In life: _____

In career: _____

In health/wellness: _____

The BIG goal I'm working towards today:

Today's priorities:

Top three mini goals:

1. _____

2. _____

3. _____

Reflection:

Today's three biggest wins:

1. _____

2. _____

3. _____

DAILY ACCOUNTABILITY

Today's mantra: I will laugh and smile as much as possible.

Date: ___ /___ /_____

Today, I am feeling:

- EXCITED
- STRESSED
- ENERGETIC
- HAPPY
- RELAXED
- RESTED
- SLEEPY
- APATHETIC
- SAD

Daily visualisation

In life: _____

In career: _____

In health/wellness: _____

```
The BIG goal I'm working towards today:



```

Today's priorities:

Top three mini goals:

1. _____

2. _____

3. _____

Reflection:

Today's three biggest wins:

1. _____

2. _____

3. _____

DAILY ACCOUNTABILITY

Today's mantra: I will go with the flow.

Date: ___ / ___ / _____

Today, I am feeling:

- EXCITED
- STRESSED
- ENERGETIC
- HAPPY
- RELAXED
- RESTED
- SLEEPY
- APATHETIC
- SAD

Daily visualisation

In life: _____

In career: _____

In health/wellness: _____

The BIG goal I'm working towards today:

Today's priorities:

Top three mini goals:

1. _____

2. _____

3. _____

Reflection:

Today's three biggest wins:

1. _____

2. _____

3. _____

WEEKLY RECAP

"I no longer force things. What flows, flows. What crashes, crashes. I only have space and energy for the things that are meant for me."

– Billy Chapata

Did I complete the past seven days?   Yes ☐   No ☐

If no, why did I miss the day/days: _____

_____

I can do better next week by: _____

_____

My best and/or biggest achievement of the week was:

_____

How is my progress is going towards your big goal?

_____

Reflection:

Some visualisation tools I used this week:

1. _____

2. _____

3. _____

My big actions for next week:

Rate your week: ___ / 10

DAILY ACCOUNTABILITY

Today's mantra: I will let go of past problems.

Date: ___ / ___ / _____

Today, I am feeling:

- EXCITED
- STRESSED
- ENERGETIC
- HAPPY
- RELAXED
- RESTED
- SLEEPY
- APATHETIC
- SAD

Daily visualisation

In life: _____

In career: _____

In health/wellness: _____

> The BIG goal I'm working towards today:

Today's priorities:

Top three mini goals:

1. _____

2. _____

3. _____

Reflection:

Today's three biggest wins:

1. _____

2. _____

3. _____

DAILY ACCOUNTABILITY

Today's mantra: I am healing myself.

Date: ___ /___ /_____

Today, I am feeling:

- EXCITED
- HAPPY
- SLEEPY
- STRESSED
- RELAXED
- APATHETIC
- ENERGETIC
- RESTED
- SAD

Daily visualisation

In life: _____

In career: _____

In health/wellness: _____

```
The BIG goal I'm working towards today:



```

Today's priorities:

Top three mini goals:

1. _____

2. _____

3. _____

Reflection:

Today's three biggest wins:

1. _____

2. _____

3. _____

DAILY ACCOUNTABILITY

Today's mantra: I will be on time.

Date: ___ / ___ / ____

Today, I am feeling:

- EXCITED
- STRESSED
- ENERGETIC
- HAPPY
- RELAXED
- RESTED
- SLEEPY
- APATHETIC
- SAD

Daily visualisation

In life: _____

In career: _____

In health/wellness: _____

The BIG goal I'm working towards today:

Today's priorities:

Top three mini goals:

1. _____

2. _____

3. _____

Reflection:

Today's three biggest wins:

1. _____

2. _____

3. _____

DAILY ACCOUNTABILITY

Today's mantra: I am loving my friends and family.

Date: ___ /___ /_____

Today, I am feeling:

- EXCITED
- HAPPY
- SLEEPY
- STRESSED
- RELAXED
- APATHETIC
- ENERGETIC
- RESTED
- SAD

Daily visualisation

In life: _____

In career: _____

In health/wellness: _____

The BIG goal I'm working towards today:

Today's priorities:

Top three mini goals:

1. _____

2. _____

3. _____

Reflection:

Today's three biggest wins:

1. _____

2. _____

3. _____

DAILY ACCOUNTABILITY

Today's mantra: I can pick and choose who I want in my life.

Date: ___ /___ /_____

Today, I am feeling:

- EXCITED
- HAPPY
- SLEEPY
- STRESSED
- RELAXED
- APATHETIC
- ENERGETIC
- RESTED
- SAD

Daily visualisation

In life: _____

In career: _____

In health/wellness: _____

The BIG goal I'm working towards today:

Today's priorities:

Top three mini goals:

1. _____

2. _____

3. _____

Reflection:

Today's three biggest wins:

1. _____

2. _____

3. _____

DAILY ACCOUNTABILITY

Today's mantra: I will provide my body with the fuel it needs.

Date: ___ /___ /_____

Today, I am feeling:

- EXCITED
- STRESSED
- ENERGETIC
- HAPPY
- RELAXED
- RESTED
- SLEEPY
- APATHETIC
- SAD

Daily visualisation

In life: _____

In career: _____

In health/wellness: _____

The BIG goal I'm working towards today:

Today's priorities:

Top three mini goals:

1. _____

2. _____

3. _____

Reflection:

Today's three biggest wins:

1. _____

2. _____

3. _____

DAILY ACCOUNTABILITY

Today's mantra: I am conscious of all my decisions.

Date: ___ / ___ / _____

Today, I am feeling:

- EXCITED
- STRESSED
- ENERGETIC
- HAPPY
- RELAXED
- RESTED
- SLEEPY
- APATHETIC
- SAD

Daily visualisation

In life: _____

In career: _____

In health/wellness: _____

The BIG goal I'm working towards today:

Today's priorities:

Top three mini goals:

1. _____

2. _____

3. _____

Reflection:

Today's three biggest wins:

1. _____

2. _____

3. _____

WEEKLY RECAP

"When you focus on problems, you'll have more problems. When you focus on possibilities, you'll have more opportunities."

– Zig Zigler

Did I complete the past seven days?   Yes ☐   No ☐

If no, why did I miss the day/days: _____

_____

I can do better next week by: _____

_____

My best and/or biggest achievement of the week was:

_____

How is my progress is going towards your big goal?

_____

Reflection:

Some visualisation tools I used this week:

1. _____

2. _____

3. _____

My big actions for next week:

Rate your week: ___ / 10

monthly review

"Don't give up now. Chances are your best kiss, your hardest laugh and your greatest day are still yet to come."

– Atticus

The single biggest/best achievement for the month was:

I'm most proud of:

My best visualisation strategy was:

Three things I loved about this month:

1. _____

2. _____

3. _____

My healthiest action was:

My best career move/decision was:

My best mindset practice was:

I felt most successful/enlightened when:

The best moment of courage I had:

A visualisation that came true was:

Three things that didn't go to plan this month:

1. _____

2. _____

3. _____

How I can avoid or improve these things next month:

1. _____

2. _____

3. _____

Three visions and actions I undertook and achieved this month:

1. _____

2. _____

3. _____

"

Be good to people. You will be remembered more for your

kindness than any level of success you could possibly gain."

– Mandy Hale

NOTES

Congratulations, you've made it to the end of your *Visions & Actions* journal!

We hope you learnt a lot about yourself and found out some common and recurring strategies that have helped you on your journey to achieving all your goals.

We hope the tools and prompts have positively affected your everyday life and everything feels more achievable, attainable and within reach (if it isn't already here!). If you'd like to continue on your Visions & Actions journey of jotting down your daily, weekly and monthly visions and achievements, grab another copy! The beauty of this wonderful little tool is that you can use it forever. You can never have too many visions! If you're anything like us, the Visions & Actions planner is a little 'thought starter' and 'butt kicker' we know we'll carry around with us forever — until the end of time!

All the best, and here's to continuing to be our best, most successful selves!

Lisa & the Collective Hub team xx

Love this journal? We think you'll really enjoy
our *Daily Gratitudes Journal*. Set out similarly to the
Visions & Actions Journal, but focusing on creating
daily habits and gratitudes.

Available from
www.collectivehub.com

Check out our other amazing journals/planners!
Including the *Create Your Best Life Journal*,
The Ultimate Guide To Social Media Marketing Journal, *The Ultimate Writer's Journal*,
and *The Ultimate Travel Journal*.

Available from
www.collectivehub.com

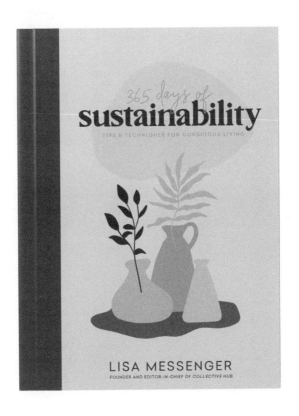

Need some inspiration on how you can do better for yourself and the world? Lisa's book, *365 Days of Sustainability*, will provide you with a tip or lesson for each day for an entire year!

Available from
www.collectivehub.com

Learn from yesterday. Cherish today.
Dream big for tomorrow.

Thoughtfully curated by entrepreneur, author and speaker Lisa Messenger, these artfully presented quotes can be used as meditations, as musings, or as your daily dose of inspiration; one for each day of the year. Every daily message includes a quote, followed by Lisa's personal take, and an affirmation that will help you to step into and ground your courage, spirit, wisdom and wit that make every day count.

Buy your copy today
www.collectivehub.com

Want to learn how to work on your own terms and live a life you love everyday? Lisa Messenger's *The Now Of Work* is jam-packed with lots of actionable advice, tips and tricks on how you can future-proof your workforce and achieve location freedom, forever!

Available from
www.collectivehub.com

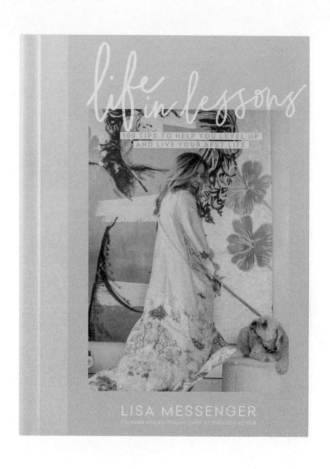

In *Life In Lessons*, Lisa shares her journey through her exciting and sometimes turbulent career, while pulling out 100 hard-hitting lessons on the way. Dip in and out or read from start to finish in this unique new format.

Available from
www.collectivehub.com

Collect all of Lisa Messenger's books!
Buy your copy at www.collectivehub.com

Want to secure a back issue of *Collective Hub* magazine? Jump online at collectivehub.com to see our full catalogue and order yours today.

> **There are three
> ways to ultimate success:
> The first way is to be kind.**